Thank God It's Monday is a great way to approach every week positively, so you can maximize the best of the week ahead. In direct sales you have to deal with a lot of rejection and failure. Surviving a week, a month or a year in direct sales isn't easy. To survive 60 plus years in sales, then, is a major achievement. This book is an opportunity to learn from one of the best—and it's priceless.

Ayo Olaseinde
President
Saladmaster, Inc.

Thank God It's Monday is an inspirational book and a philosophy on life that is for everyone, not just the sales professional. With his personal stories of trials and triumph, it is easy to see why he has been the success he is. While some measure success in financial terms, the impact Larry has had on people lives around the world is the true measure of success. *Thank God It's Monday* is that philosophy, which in its simplicity, is a recipe that can provide anyone with the same success as Larry. I am grateful to have been able to learn first-hand from Larry over the years, and now I'm glad everyone else can, too.

Ryan C. Reigle
Senior Vice President, Sales
Saladmaster, Inc.

Larry's latest book is a unique twist on loving life and business sooo much, he can't wait to start the week over again...and again! This level of passion has fueled him to build a sales organization that has been stack ranked in the TOP of his industry, for over 50 years! Imagine tapping into the wisdom and genius of one of the foremost direct sellers who ever lived. And imagine yourself duplicating that level of enthusiasm for decades and decades!

James Tanti, Area VP, MD
Saladmaster, Inc.

Larry has hit a home run with this book. It's an exciting journey both in both the sales and spiritual realms.

Wayne A. Fritz
Senior Vice President
Saladmaster, Inc.

THANK
GOD
IT'S
MONDAY!

May the Lord
Bless You

LARRY DICKMAN

x

Archway Publishing books may be ordered
through booksellers or by contacting:

Archway Publishing
1663 Liberty Drive
Bloomington, IN 47403
www.archwaypublishing.com
844-669-3957

Because of the dynamic nature of the Internet, any web addresses or
links contained in this book may have changed since publication and
may no longer be valid. The views expressed in this work are solely those
of the author and do not necessarily reflect the views of the publisher,
and the publisher hereby disclaims any responsibility for them.

Any people depicted in stock imagery provided by Getty Images are
models, and such images are being used for illustrative purposes only.
Certain stock imagery © Getty Images.

Interior Image Credit: Phil Garza

ISBN: 978-1-4808-9736-6 (sc)
ISBN: 978-1-4808-9737-3 (e)

Library of Congress Control Number: 2020919441

Print information available on the last page.

Archway Publishing rev. date: 12/22/2020

DEDICATION

This book is dedicated to all salespeople, but especially to the direct salespeople who are out on the streets searching for prospects (which we fondly call "prospecting"). Without salesmen and saleswomen this world would be without—and I do mean without—the very foundation of our economy. From the farmer to the grocery store, to the auto industry to the stock market, sales are an inseparable part of the equation. Salespeople, in short, keep this world running. To you, I dedicate this book.

To my Estherbrook family who are the most professional salespeople I know.

To the Saladmaster salespeople worldwide; you have encouraged me to write this book. May you be blessed as you have blessed me.

To my beautiful wife Elaine, who has spent endless hours home alone as I have been writing this book and traveling the world. Thank you, my Elaine, for the many prayers for my safety and inspiration.

And most importantly to my Heavenly Father, who through the inspiration of the Holy Spirit filled my mind with the thoughts for this little book. I only pray that I have interpreted His voice correctly, and that you, the reader, will find some fresh motivation within its pages.

Larry Dickman
August 1, 2020

CONTENTS

INTRODUCTION

Welcome to Monday

Thank God for Monday.

Thank God for a new week, new beginnings, and new opportunities.

Throughout my working life I have heard the expression, "Thank God it's Friday." TGIF! Some people even say, "Thank God for Wednesday," because it puts them that much closer to Friday.

Why is Friday such an important day? For many, it's the end of the work week, and that is cause enough for celebration.

But if we celebrate the end of a week, why not celebrate the beginning?

Monday is a God-given opportunity to begin again. And the most important Monday-morning-attitude you can have is to leave last week in last week. Don't carry the failures and hurts of the last seven days into the next seven days. Don't clutter up a brand-new week with yesterday's failures, hurts and disappointments.

I sometimes think back to the creation account in Genesis, the first book of the Bible. The record tells us that God created the world in seven days. Were they literal, 24hour days? I can't tell you for sure, because I wasn't there. But that's what the Bible says, and I have no problem with it at all. After all, He is God, the Almighty, and He can do anything He pleases. He could have created everything in 24 seconds if He had chosen to.

If Sunday was the first day of His creation week, that's the day Genesis tells us created light, and divided it from the darkness. Wow. Light! Something that had not existed on earth to that point. I would say that was a good day's work, wouldn't you? I would like to be able to come home at night, have my wife ask me, "How did your day go?" and tell her, "It went very well. I created light today."

On the second day, Monday, He created the sky. The sky! Think of all the beautiful skies you have seen in your lifetime. A misty spring morning out in the country with the sun breaking through. Or how about a golden sunset at Ala Moana Beach Park on Oahu? Picture a deep blue summer sky from your childhood. The sky is wonderful beyond words. Who but God could have created sky?

What was there before the sky? I don't know. But Genesis 1:7 says that "God made a dome, and it separated the water from under it from the water above it. He named the dome 'Sky.' Evening passed and morning came—that was the second day."[1] That was Monday.

On Monday, God made the sky.

Do you think God was excited about that Monday? I think He was. The night before, Sunday night, there had been no sky. No deep blue dome overhead. No floating clouds. No canvas for the billions of magnificent sunrises and sunsets that were to come.

God was excited about Monday. He had no desire to skip quickly to Friday so He could say "TGIF." He loved to create and He loved Monday, at the very beginning of His creation.

And I would simply say to you, "Wake up to Monday. Your whole life is before you.

Opportunities unimagined are before you.

You were not born to be a failure. God created you special—like no one else.

Genesis 2:14 tells us that God created Man in His own image, and right out of the box He gave Him a very important job. He was to name the animals. God gave him power to rule over the creation.

With God's help, you have the power to rule over last week's mistakes. You, yes *you*. You have the power to succeed. Just move into your Monday with an "I can do it" attitude.

God built new days, new weeks, new months, and new years into the very fabric of His creation. There are so many opportunities to begin again!

In the pages of this little book, I want to talk about

my career in sales—and maybe your career, too. You only have one life on earth, so you have to be careful and wise about how you invest it. I'm just here to say I'm happy I invested it as a salesman.

Wouldn't change a thing.

And I still love Mondays.

1

THE BOOT

IT WAS A COLD, RAINY NIGHT IN THE WILLAMETTE Valley. I was home with my father on one of the rare evenings when he wasn't sitting in the local bar, drinking away what little income he made working on the hop ranch where we lived. Fortunately, the farmer had provided us with a place to eat and sleep.

But it wasn't much. Hardly more than an 18-by-20-foot one-room shack.

On one side of the room was a wrought-iron bed with a bed spring and a stinky, threadbare mattress. A big, cut-open hop sack curtained off our sleeping area. The tiny cabin had an old pot-bellied wood stove where we could cook our meals, a small wooden table, and two rickety wood chairs.

A single, bare light bulb hung on a wire from the ceiling, providing our only light.

As I said, it wasn't much. But it was home until I joined the Navy at 17.

But this particular rainy night in the cabin was different, and that's why it lingers in my memory. For some reason, Dad stayed home with me that evening. It was an exceptionally dark and dreary night—damp and cold—and I was very glad of his company. The rain drumming on the board-and-tar-paper roof made a lonesome sound. It was one of the only times I can remember when my dad and I bonded a little as father and son.

It isn't much to remember, is it? But at least I have something.

The only other furniture in the cabin were two worn out car seats—and the stove to keep us warm. If we put too much wood in it to heat up our shack the tin stove and stovepipe would glow red, with the danger of catching the roof on fire. So we kept our fires small, and huddled near the stove for warmth.

"Watch the stove pipe," I remember my dad saying. "Don't let it get too red."

It was 1946. The Great Depression had pretty much slowed down, and most of the nation was now back to work, mostly due to the second world war.

I was 12 years old, and it had been several years since my mother left us. I remember sitting near the stove, trying to carve a cowboy boot with an old pocket knife my father had given me. The knife wouldn't hold a good edge, and had to be sharpened over and over again.

I was whittling on some castoff pieces of lumber. After several attempts, my dad showed me how a boot should look. In my first go-around, I had the top of the boot creased sideways instead of facing forward, the way a cowboy boot should look like.

At that age and time, most young boys in America admired the cowboys they would see at the movies or listen to on the radio shows. They wanted to be like their heroes, Gene Autry, Roy Rogers, Hop Along Cassidy or the Lone Ranger. I remember how I had somehow scraped together enough money to buy a cap pistol—a shiny replica of a cowboy's trusty .44 caliber. I must have worked for hours on my fast draw!

But cowboys weren't just in the movies. At that time, there were still plenty of real, working cowboys in the Western United States, and wild horses still roamed the plans.

My father was born at a time of great change in the world. Cars were just becoming popular, although not everyone could afford one. In the little farm where I was born, however, we had no electricity or indoor plumbing. Our "bathroom" was a little privy behind the house. I didn't experience the luxury of toilet paper until I was in the eighth grade. We used a Sears-Roebuck or Montgomery Wards catalog for that purpose, and no, it certainly wasn't Charmin.

My father drowned his sorrows with alcohol most every night, but I was hurting, too. My mother had been out of my life for three years, but I still missed her, and had no idea where she was or how to contact her. We had no phone and there were no letters.

I often thought about running away as I would lay awake on that old mattress, worrying about my father, wondering what he was doing out so late at night, and if he would be able to make it home on his own. In the distance, I could hear the big Southern Pacific steam engines chugging through the valley, their whistles echoing in the night, and the clattering line of boxcars trailing behind.

Many a time I thought about leaving my bed and catching one of those boxcars, heading off into who-knows-where. I had no idea where those trains were going, but that didn't matter. I just wanted to escape the pain, hunger and loneliness. But I knew I couldn't. I knew it was my duty was to stay with my father, no matter how unhappy the situation might be. What if he couldn't find his way home one night? Who would look for him? Who would care?

In those days I imagined that a career as a hobo riding the rails would be a good prospect for me, and offer all the adventure I could long for. But that wasn't what God in His grace had in mind for me. By His wonderful love and kindness, I have been able to achieve everything in life I could have ever dreamed of. I've enjoyed the blessings of a wife and home, and in my career as a direct salesperson, I've been privileged to visit some strange and wonderful places across the globe.

I've had the opportunity to live comfortably, and enjoy some luxuries in life I could have never imagined in that leaky little shack in the Willamette Valley. But most of all, I've had the privilege to share this rich and interesting vocation with others, men and women who are looking for new opportunities and a chance to succeed in a challenging and rewarding career.

As direct salespeople, we have the opportunity to become very successful, and eventually earn a lot of money. (If you invest it right, you can live very comfortably.) But it is also important to remember your roots, and not forget the blessings that have come your way.

I still have that old wooden boot I whittled under a single 60-watt light bulb that night with my dad, and of all the worldly things that my Lord has blessed me with, that carving means more to me than all of them. When I look at it, I remember how far the Lord has brought me and the doors He has opened for me. I've been able to share financial blessings with many who live in third world countries, as well as here at home.

Today I have all that anyone could ask for, but I must never forget where I started, and how, and why I am blessed.

2

YOUR LEGACY

AFTER OVER SIX DECADES IN THE HARNESS, I'M still in love with direct selling.

I remember the old Elvis tune "All Shook Up" from my youth, and I still feel that way about my chosen career. A famous coffee company once had the slogan, "Wake up to life." A lot of people get their eyes open with coffee every morning (I personally prefer tea), but it's even more important to wake up to a day you really *want* to live. After all these years I still want to throw the covers back in the morning and walk into the new day. Am I walking a little more slowly? Yes. But I still have the expectation that somehow, even in some small way, I will have the opportunity to change someone's life for the better.

Is that my legacy? Or part of it? I hope so. God helping me, it will be.

The dictionary defines "legacy" as a gift of money or personal property. But it's much more than that, isn't it? It is also something handed down from one generation to generations that follow. Leaving a financial legacy for your children and grandchildren can be a warmly welcomed event and perhaps a great blessing. But it may not be the *best* thing you could pass along to those who follow you. It's even more important to leave them with an example, an inspiration, a life story that will be remembered and perhaps even treasured through the years.

As I was pondering all this, some famous names and legacies came immediately to mind. Whenever a celebrated figure dies, we speak much about the legacy of that person. We share their resume of beloved books, music, or films. We speak of their accomplishments in making the world a better place, their contributions to humanity, or the simple pleasures they brought into many lives. We honor them by our attention to, and appreciation of what they left behind.

Here are just a few examples.

SAMUEL LONGHORN CLEMENS

Known to us by his penname, Mark Twain, Clemens was an author, humorist, entrepreneur, publisher, and lecturer. Yet none of his accomplishments stand out more than his two classic novels about life on the Mississippi River: *The Adventures of Tom Sawyer* and *The Adventures of Huckleberry Finn*. Drawing on stories and characters from his own colorful youth, Clemens left us with a rich experience of early American boyhood and pulled back the curtain on an era in our history that will never come again. I especially like his recorded comment that "Twenty years from now, you will be more disappointed by the things you didn't do, than by the ones you did."[2]

THOMAS EDISON

This man left a legacy of many practical inventions that touch our lives in a thousand ways. These include the phonograph, photographic film, the incandescent light bulb, the movie camera, and even electric power distribution. Think of how many ways this man's inventions shape our world every day—and we never give it a second thought! Every time you turn on a light in your house, you experience part of our heritage from this visionary genius. In my own life, that legacy extended to our little shack on the hop ranch, with the single bulb hanging on a wire from the ceiling.

SIR WINSTON CHURCHILL

On October 29, 1941, during the Second World War, Churchill spoke over the BBC to his island nation. In the face of waves of Nazi bombers blasting English cities, Churchill told the listening nation to never give up and never give in.

He repeated the word never three times, to make sure they got the message. The might of the enemy at that time looked almost overwhelming, but the Prime Minister challenged every man, woman, and child on the island to stand firm. Churchill never did give up, and neither did the United Kingdom. It is his legacy to all of us. Apart from him, we might be living in a very different world.

Will this be your legacy, too? Will you like Sir Winston determine to never give up or give in, no matter how dark it gets? I have overcome many adversities that should have put me into bankruptcy—or worse—had it not been for my faith in God and my excitement for the future, with all its unknowns and possibilities. If you have a dream, then determine here and now to never give up on your dream. Even when the cloud of disappointment hovers over you. Never, never, give up.

GENERAL DOUGLAS MACARTHUR

Just a year later, during that same horrendous world war, U.S. Army General MacArthur made a strong declaration to the people of the Philippines as their islands were being overrun by the powerful and vicious Japanese Imperial Army. The American and Allied forces were forced to retreat from the Philippines, but MacArthur declared, "I shall return!" And he did. On October 20, 1944, he came back and drove the enemy soldiers from those shores.

Just recently I met a survivor of that conflict. She was just a young girl during that war, and she shared with me her memories of running and hiding with her mother, always looking for food. She told me how they hid in the jungle and lived off the land, eating bugs or roots or whatever they could find.

My stepfather was Filipino, and his stories of those agonizing days helped me to feel the pain of a nation beaten, raped, and brutalized by soldiers who had no mercy. He told me about the Filipino freedom fighters, hopelessly outmanned and outgunned, who fought back against the invaders for years, making lightning quick raids and then slipping back into the jungle. They held on against overwhelming odds, because they had a promise from the American general: "I shall return." He kept his promise and that became his legacy.

Keeping your promises, to your spouse, to your children, to your friends, and to your God is one of the finest legacies you could ever leave.

LOU HOLTZ

Holtz was the legendary coach of the Notre Dame football team for 11-seasons, between 1986 and 1996. During one stretch, his Fighting Irish teams won 23 straight games. But he was more than a great football strategist, he was and is a motivator and an inspirational speaker. Among his many memorable quotes, here are a few of my favorites:

"When all is said and done, more is said than done."

"Don't be a spectator, don't let life pass you by."

"Ability is what you're capable of doing. Motivation determines what you do. Attitude determines how well you do it."

"Do right. Do your best. Treat others as you want to be treated."

And finally: *"Chase your dreams."*[3]

I really like that last quote. All great accomplishments start with a dream. Dreams fuel your enthusiasm and vision. They give you a burning desire to get up in the morning, do your best, persevere and achieve. (Remember, Edison had to dream about a light bulb before he ever figured out how to build one. No one in all the universe had ever seen a light bulb, until Edison saw it in his dream.)

ELVIS PRESSLEY

In my first Saladmaster convention in Las Vegas, our company president Harry Lemons was warning everyone stay away from the slots. But the slots really weren't the main attraction at the time. It was Elvis! He had a big show going at that time on The Strip. My wife Elaine begged and pleaded with me to go see him, but I knew we couldn't afford the tickets. I was just starting my career, and the whole trip to Vegas was already pushing our meager finances to the limit. So we didn't go, and we never got to see Elvis. And now, of course, I wish I'd found a way to do it.

Elvis was one of the pioneers of rock n' roll, and before too many years, he was crowned its unofficial King. He did make some movies, but he will be remembered mostly for his groundbreaking popular music.

Presley grew up dirt-poor in Tupelo, Mississippi and moved with his family to Memphis when he was 13. He was a small-town country boy who probably never even dreamed of worldwide fame.

What was his legacy? Was it his leather outfits with sequins, his disjointed hips, his electric personality, or the jukebox tunes that worked their way into the collective memories of multiple generations? Who could forget songs like "Jailhouse Rock,"

"Heartbreak Hotel," or "Love Me Tender" bouncing

around the airwaves in the 1950s and 1960s? Elvis died of a heart attack (following years of prescription drug abuse) at age the of 42, but in his brief life he had become an American icon as recognizable as the Statue of Liberty or Mount Rushmore Very few of us will leave a legacy as memorable as that. But does it really matter? If we are able to influence, inspire or encourage even a small group of family, friends and strangers in the course of our lives, that sounds like pretty good stewardship to me.

MARTIN LUTHER KING, JR.

Everyone remembers Dr. King for his "I have a dream" speech that he gave before 200,000 people in Washington D.C., on August 28, 1963. It was a cry for justice and equality that echoed across America, around the world, and ended up in the history books. Even though his dream eventually led him to his death, his legacy of courage lives on for the world to see. Streets in our cities and a holiday on our calendars honor his name.

Has his dream been fully accomplished in America? Some say yes, and some say no. But no one can argue about the impact of his life. And it all began, as so many vital and important things do, with a dream.

What is your legacy? Your legacy is about you. It's about what you have accomplished in your lifetime, and how you will be remembered by family and friends and even strangers in the years to come.

No, you may not save Great Britain like Churchill, write a symphony like Beethoven, invent something that becomes indispensable like Edison, or launch a nation-changing movement like Martin Luther King, Jr. You may never even have your name in the paper, except at your birth and passing. It may boil down to something kind you did for someone along the way. It may not have seemed like such an extraordinary act or big event to you at the time. You might not even remember it.

One of my friends was telling me how a lady had searched out his email and wrote to him "out of the blue." Apparently, some 25 years before, he had given this woman a quiet word of encouragement after a church service. My friend had no memory of the woman or of the incident. But she wrote to him to say, "You have no idea how your words helped me that day. I've remembered them all these years."

My friend had left a little legacy, a little part of himself, even though he hadn't been aware of it.

And that makes me think of Mark Benson.

A LEGACY OF KINDNESS

I will always remember a former Saladmaster dealer named Mark Benson, for the kindness he and his wife Lela showed my wife and me when we were new in the business. When we met them at the conventions, they would invite us out for ice cream. If we happened to be in Salt Lake City, they would invite us over to their home. Over the years, we became very close to their family.

Whether they realize it or not, that investment in our lives will always be a part of Mark and Lela Benson's legacy. And I am sure that influence extends to many, many more people. They set an example for Elaine and me, and left us with many grateful memories.

Legacy is a small word with only six letters, but it can carry more meaning than we might ever imagine.

So just to set the stage, how do you want to be remembered? What do you want to be your legacy? Will you be remembered for your acts of kindness—or perhaps even sacrifice? When your name surfaces in some future conversation, will you be recalled as a trustworthy, faithful, honest person? Will people speak of you as a visionary, or someone who held to your course after setbacks or heartbreak?

Maybe you haven't given these things much thought. It might be something in the back of your mind, that doesn't occupy much of your attention. Maybe you are too busy working and living to think about your influence. Nevertheless, you *do* have influence, and you *will* leave a legacy—of one kind or another.

I want mine to be one that makes people smile, or maybe keep getting up and getting back into the race after being sidelined or knocked down. The simple fact is, apart from God's grace and help my success would be empty and my legacy not worth remembering.

But here is the key. You need to be thinking about your legacy right now, today, and not after you are laid six feet under. When your name appears in the obituary column of your local papers, it will be too late to go back and correct what you should have done right.

A FEW MORE EXAMPLES

Chris Nathatis, in Boston, was one of the first Saladmaster salespeople to ever go on TV with an infomercial. He was a natural, and became something of a celebrity in that part of the country. No one had ever done what he did in front of the camera, banging an inferior aluminum cooking pan against a Saladmaster pan, with its three-play 18.8 stainless steel, proving that this cookware was indestructible. Because of his magnetic personality and notoriety, he was headlined in state fairs with hundreds coming to see him do cooking demos on stage.

He was one of the first in our business to use the TV medium, and his legacy paved the way for many others that would follow.

I think of Zig Ziglar, one of our own who stepped out by faith and began sharing his insights and experiences with a much wider audience. Always a salesman's salesman, Ziglar was also a man of faith who spoke to countless thousands of people and produced bestselling books and motivational tapes. It is estimated the Ziglar influenced a quarter of a billion people through his 33 books, including the bestseller,

See You at the Top, which has sold almost two million copies.[4]

Those books and tapes have carried me through

many hard times, helping me close many sales, and teaching me the important of prospecting.

Leaving a legacy grows out of a desire to be remembered for what you have contributed to the world—or to be more specific, *your* world. I'm talking about the people who have known you, interacted with you, walked with you, loved you, or perhaps even competed against you. You and I may never be known outside of a modest circle of colleagues, family members and acquaintances. But what we do *within* that circle, how we make a difference right where we are, will leave a lasting footprint.

You hope your life matters in some way. I know I do. So, carve your name on hearts, not tombstones. A legacy is etched into the minds of others and the stories they share about you when you're gone. That legacy of your love will live on.

I can't help but think about a woman in the New Testament who left a powerful legacy. And we don't even know her name.

Just hours away from going to the cross, Jesus and His disciples were having a meal in the home of a friend. As they were eating, an unnamed woman approached with a precious jar of alabaster, filled to the brim with expensive perfume. Humbly and lovingly, she poured it out on the Lord's head. Several of the disciples went berserk. They turned on her in anger and said, "Why this waste of perfume? You should have sold it and given the money to the poor!"

But Jesus would have none of that. Defending the woman, He said, "Leave her alone.... Why are you bothering her? She has done a beautiful thing to me. The poor you will always have with you, and you can help them any time you want. But you will not always have me. She did what she could. She poured perfume on my body beforehand to prepare for my burial."

Then, perhaps looking at the woman who had sacrificed so much, He said, "Truly I tell you, wherever the gospel is preached throughout the world, what she has done will also be told, in memory of her." (See Mark 14:6-9.)

In that moment, Jesus gave her an incredible legacy. For the next 2,000 years, in possibly every country around the world, this woman's simple act of love and sacrifice has been told, retold, and pondered—by millions! She left a legacy of generosity, sacrifice, worship and love. It was just a simple, possibly impulsive gesture that was over in 60 seconds. But here we are, 20 centuries later, still thinking about it. What she did for her Lord will roll on forever.

Each of us needs to spend time reflecting on what is most important in our lives. What we accomplish for ourselves with our talents, experience, and sheer determination may bring us real satisfaction in the days and years to come.

But it is what we do for others that will be remembered.

3

FIRST STEPS

EVERY JOURNEY—WHETHER A THOUSAND MILES OR a few steps—begins somewhere.

My particular journey began on a small, non-productive farm outside the little town of Hammond, Minnesota. My father came here from Germany, with his parents, and my mother from French-speaking Montreal.

My father spoke German, my mother spoke French, and everyone else I knew spoke English, so, yes, I had some trouble sorting it all out. From there we moved to a log cabin in the mountains of Tennessee, where my father built such cabins as summer homes for the wealthy.

Our next stop was the Willamette Valley in Oregon, where we lived in a tent village, and my dad tried to get work in one of the canneries. (You can read the rest of my life story in my first book, *A Salesman.*)

My spiritual journey had a beginning point, too, and means even more to me. In 1953 I was in the Navy studying underwater demolition at Treasure Island Naval Base, near San Francisco.

I was 19 years old, and nearly eaten up with anxiety. Day and night, it seemed troubling questions kept running through my brain. What if I blew myself up or drowned? What would happen to me if I died? Would my body be buried somewhere in an unmarked grave—or possibly buried at sea and become fish food? I was young, healthy, and gainfully employed, but I had no peace.

As I told in more detail in my earlier book, the fear of death was upon me, and I didn't know what to do or where to turn. The only prayer I could remember was the one my mother taught me as a little boy, before she left my dad and me.

Lying in my bunk at night I prayed, "*Now I lay me down to sleep. I pray the Lord my soul to keep. If I should die before I wake, I pray the Lord my soul take.*" I was so afraid of death that I would pray it in the morning, too, and sometimes under my breath through the day. It wasn't much of a prayer, but it was all I knew.

I imagine that some of my shipmates during those days thought I was losing my mind. I went to see the chaplain, thinking that if anyone had the answers it would be him. But I went away disappointed. His answers were rambling and vague, and he couldn't seem to give me any reassurance. Still seeking, I attended a few Mormon Bible studies, but they couldn't give me any hope for the future, either. No one seemed to have any word for me that would ease my fear of death.

So I kept praying that little prayer my mother had taught me. At some point, I remembered the New Testament at the bottom of my sea bag; I dug it out and began to read in it whenever I had the spare time.

That's when I found out I'd had the answers I wanted all along. It was all right there in that little New Testament I had hidden away so no one else could see.

One day I was reading in the little book of First John, these words suddenly jumped out at me:

> *If we confess our sins, He is faithful and
> just to forgive us our sins, and to cleanse us
> from all unrighteousness. (1 John 1:9, NKJV)*

I remember reading that verse and feeling stunned. There it was! Just what I had been looking for. It was as if a light came on, shining over all of the questions and fears that had darkened my heart for so many weeks. Suddenly, it was all very clear to me. If I confessed my sins to God, He was faithful and just to forgive me, because of Jesus. At that very moment I *knew* that if I died, I would be home in heaven with my heavenly Father, and with Jesus.

So now I had a new prayer—and a better one. As I confessed my sins to the Father in Jesus' name, He promised to make me clean and whole. It was so exciting to me! My relationship with God began to develop from that day, and I began devoting more and more time to reading my little New Testament, day and night.

So this is where my most important journey began. It was as if a bright light had flicked on in my mind, and all my doubts and fears vanished like a bad dream.

Writing it now, it sounds like a cliché. But it really happened. My whole world had changed almost overnight. One of the first lessons that I learned was if I was willing to allow the Holy Spirit to have control of my life (rather than me), unexpected and wonderful things would take place. No one had ever taught me about this "Holy Spirit"—whom Jesus referred to as our Guide, Advocate, Teacher, and Comforter—but I remember how He began to speak to me in quiet moments. There was no audible voice, but I knew without question that those new thoughts and plans and directions weren't coming from my own brain.

But then I heard something that made no sense at all.

God seemed to be saying to me (over and over again) "I want you to go back to Japan, and speak to people in the bars about Me."

It seemed insane. How in the world could that even happen? I remember saying right out loud, "Lord, the Navy controls my life! I can't just up and go." When I had finished my training, I was expecting orders to go somewhere to use my training. But that's not what happened.

I was handed new orders—and could hardly believe what I was reading. I was being put on a transport ship bound for Japan! In fact, I was being sent back to the very town where I had lived before beginning my training. It was an answer to the words the Lord had spoken to me about, but at the moment I couldn't see that. And I wasn't happy at all about being stuck on a slow ship to Yokohama.

God, of course, had orchestrated the very thing I thought could never happen. I had told Him (out loud) that it couldn't happen because "the Navy controls my life." But it wasn't true. The *Lord* was in control of my life, and He was moving me right where He wanted me to be.

Several days later, as the slow old ship plodded its way across the Pacific Ocean, I was walking toward the stern of the ship after breakfast when I saw several sailors sitting next to a ladder going to the upper deck. They were studying the Bible. One again, I heard that now-familiar voice saying to me, *I want you to go and study with them.*

Study the Bible? On a Navy ship in the middle of the ocean? But what about my duties? Once again, I saw how God could orchestrate events in my life. For whatever reason, I wasn't given any duties that would hinder me from those Bible studies. This went on for the whole time it took us the sail to Yokohama.

Just before we were to arrive in port, I went back to the place where we met at the usual time to say goodbye to these guys. But there was no one there. I asked all over the ship about them—and it wasn't a huge ship—but no one knew them. No one had seen them. Not even the sailors who had walked right past the place where we would study every day!

Who were those guys who taught this young sailor from the Bible?

I will let you draw your own conclusions.

You can read about my further adventures, including the highs and the lows, back in Japan in *A Salesman*. I made my share of mistakes, sins, and foolish decisions in those days, but that wonderful verse—1 John 1:9— assured me that I could confess those sins and find forgiveness with God. In the times when I felt weakest and most like a failure, I would call out to God and find a power working in me beyond what I could have imagined.

A NEW DIRECTION

Thank God it's Monday! My introduction to the work week began after being honorably discharged from the Navy. I married Elaine at age 21, and began work as a carwash boy for a car dealership in Walla Walla, Washington. I was taking home all of 45 dollars a week at that time, but was glad for the opportunity, and glad to be out of the Navy.

After a few days on the job, I found out that another young man working for the same dealership had found a way to supplement his income.

He'd found a sales job.

Come to find out, he was selling a program called a "food freezer plan," and his weekly sales income was more than I was making in a whole month. That definitely got my attention. I remember thinking to myself, *He's no smarter than I am. And he doesn't have all that much personality. Yet he has found a way to increase his income while I'm still washing and polishing cars for 45 bucks per week. There is something wrong with this picture!*

So I asked my friend to introduce me to his manager.

This wasn't quite my first introduction to sales. Technically, my first job was selling newspapers at age 12. But this was definitely a huge step in my life journey.

The manager turned out to be the owner, and he was willing to give a rookie kid a chance. "Just watch and learn," he told me. That was good advice then, and it is still good advice today.

This sales job, however, didn't last very long. Customers who had bought into the program came up short on food before it was time to reorder. Complaints started pouring in, and I didn't know how to deal with them. Then I found out that the owner was buying the freezer foods wholesale, and selling them for more than the retail stores were selling the same food. (The customers found out about that, too.)

It was time to move on. But the experience hadn't been wasted. One thing I had learned from the get-go was how to search for prospects. "Prospecting" was the way to get succeed in sales and appointments, and it still is.

The other thing I learned early in my sales career was how to get bookings from my presentations; the more appointments I got from my prospects, the less prospecting I had to do.

My next sale job was selling encyclopedias, and that lasted all of one week. I had canvassed an area all week to get one appointment. The sales manager had told me that if I could land an appointment, he would teach me what to say. If a sale resulted, he said that he would pay me 50 dollars. We did get the sale, and I got paid when we left the house.

But I didn't like how he had misrepresented the facts to the customer. He told them things that we both knew weren't true. So as soon as we stepped out onto the sidewalk, I handed him the briefcase, told him thank you for the opportunity, and went on my way. Even in those days when we really needed the income, I didn't want to compromise my integrity just to get a sale. And I still don't.

From there, I want to selling a cookware line. I found that I really enjoyed selling items for the kitchen (a hint of things to come), but once again I didn't like the exaggerations and outright untruths they wanted me to say. The product was good, all right, but it wasn't *that* good. And compromising my Christian faith certainly wasn't a price I was willing to pay.

The next sales job was good one; I went to work selling retail appliances for a department store chain called the Bon Marche—long since bought out by Macy's.

Archie, the department manager, really took me under his wing and taught me how to be forthright and honest in my presentations. I've always looked back on that job as the real beginning of my sales career.

In those days selling was looked down on as a shabby, maybe even shady way to earn a living. With what I had experienced already in my brief career, I could see why people felt that way. But that wasn't for me. I made up my mind to stick to the facts about the product and only tell the truth, letting the chips fall where they may. I determined right then and there that I would do everything in my power, as far as it depended on me, to change that perception of sales. And that has been my lifelong goal.

As the years have rolled along, I have seen attitudes toward direct selling change for the better. It has now become an acceptable—even desirable—profession, and I for one am proud to be part of that culture.

AN INTRODUCTION TO SALADMASTER

After a stint of selling Singer Sewing Machines at a little store in Richland, Washington, I went back to selling cookware in 1965.

One day when I arrived at a young woman's house for a demo appointment, I found that a representative from a rival cookware firm was already there, doing a demonstration of his own. Instead of getting upset about the awkward situation, I decided to see what I could learn, and quietly sat down to watch his technique.

He was a small Filipino man, and he was enthusiastically showing this young lady about a special little valve on the pan's lid. It went click-click-click as it released steam from the boiling water.

Drawn into the presentation in spite of myself, I said, "What's that clicking sound?" "It's called a Vapo Valve,™" he told me.

A light went on in my mind, and I immediately saw the possibilities of this innovation. Luster Craft, the brand I'd been selling, didn't have that feature.

I asked the representative what company he worked for.

"Saladmaster," he said with a smile—as if knowing that he had a superior product and had me beat from the get-go. I found out that the company was located in Dallas, Texas, and that very day I sat down and called them.

Who should answer the phone but Harry Lemons himself, the founder and owner of the company!

I explained to him how I had watched the cookware demo, that I was currently selling Luster Craft, and that I was interested in a dealership—right away. In no time at all, he'd sent one of his managers out to the Northwest and signed me up.

Harry told me that the regional manager would get me up to speed with all the Saladmaster programs, and train me how to use their products. I was happy about that.

A day or so with the regional manager was just what I had hoped for.

Unfortunately, he didn't see it that way.

He came into town on a Saturday morning, and asked me to join him for breakfast. Then, after 30 minutes, he shook my hand and he was gone.

There would be no training. I was on my own.

If I wanted to sell Saladmaster, I would have to rely on my previous cookware experience, and try to integrate the features and benefits of the new product line into my presentation.

But it was worse than that.

Knowing I was green in the business and needed financing, the regional manager set up an arrangement that allowed him to skim off my profits and take credit for my sales.

Cashing in on all my work, he had even "won" a sales contest, allowing him to travel with the company president on a hunting trip to Alaska.

Boy...was I ever discouraged.

When Harry Lemons got wind of this, however, he quickly corrected the problem and set matters right. I kept on doing what I knew I was good at, and that was prospecting and demonstrating how this wonderful product would bring joy and delight into any kitchen, beginning with the very first meal.

Why do I tell this story? It's really just an illustration of the hardships, setbacks and disappointments all of us face in life—no matter what our chosen career.

There will always be greedy and dishonest people out there, looking for ways to take advantage of others, seeking to climb the success ladder by walking over other people along the way. But we can't let those things, no matter how big or small, to get in the way of achieving our dreams. We must keep doing what is right, and we must keep pressing forward.

And so much good has happened to balance out those hard times! When I started at Saladmaster there were only 35 dealers, including myself. And now there are dealerships with thousands of consultants all over the world. And there is unlimited opportunity for growth

4

CONVENTIONS AND OTHER ADVENTURES

I N MY EARLY YEARS AS A DEALER, IT WAS TRIAL AND error, and probably more error than trial. By staying mostly positive, however, and holding onto my "never give up" determination, I was able to make a good living. Even so, achieving my dreams was still quite a ways down the road.

One of the most eye-opening moments in my early career happened at a Saladmaster convention in Las Vegas in 1970. I had been reading about a young man in the company who had ordered a brand-new Lincoln Mark III, and made enough sales in just 90 days to pay cash for the car.

Now that got my attention. I wanted to meet this young salesman and learn his secrets. I was especially interested in finding how he was able to do so many cooking shows and still manage to cover his callbacks. I hadn't been doing so well in that department, and it was a frustration to me.

His name was Paul Rush, and Harry Lemons had asked him to be the guest speaker at the convention. I wanted to meet the gentleman who was successful enough to pay cash for this beautiful car.

The first thing Elaine and I did was to invite young Paul to sit at our table one night at dinner. That's when I sprang my big question. How was he able to schedule five to six shows per week and keep up on his callbacks?

His answer stunned me.

"I don't make callbacks," he said. "But here is what I do. At my cooking shows I hold up a square griddle and say, 'The first one to order tonight gets this griddle. Free.'" With that, he got up and left our table.

What? That was his big secret? I could have rung his

neck. "There has to be more than that!" I told Elaine. I was so disappointed. One of the main reasons we had scraped together the money to attend the convention was so I could meet Paul Rush.

But for whatever reason, he wasn't in the mood to share a little of his success.

"That's it," I told Elaine. "I don't know how he does it, but I can't pull it off like him. I'll have to cancel my shows and go back to my old callback program."

Elaine, however, being the wife that she is, said, "Why don't you just try it?" And I did.

FIRST PITCH

When I got home, I went to my first show I had booked before I left for the convention.

To say I was nervous would be a huge understatement.

When Yogi Berra talked about being nervous, he said, "I always get nervous the nights we played in the World Series. First pitch, I was nervous. Then after that, forget it; I'd start playing."[5]

So, for me, this was the World Series, and I was standing at the plate, waiting for that first pitch. I plunged in.

When the time came to close the sales, I followed the example of Paul Rush. Holding up on 11-inch square griddle, I said, "The first person to place their order tonight gets this griddle. Who will be first?"

Three hands shot up simultaneously.

Oh great, I thought. *Now what?* I had to give each one of them a griddle with their orders. Paul had been right about getting a response. He just hadn't explained wat to do about multiple prize winners.

It wasn't the smoothest of presentations, and I wasn't nearly as effective and smoothly professional as I had wanted to be. But it was a start—and I had to admit that it I'd had some fun. I held onto all my bookings for that month. On one night alone, I sold 13 sets. And the callback plan was working for me, too, in spite of what the brilliant Paul Rush had said. One night I wrote orders for 11 sets.

On most weeks, however, when I would cook for five nights in a row, my goal was to deliver five sets a week. Exceeding that goal was a thrill.

THE KEY THAT DIDN'T FIT

Another great convention I like to remember from the early 1970s was in Nashville, Tennessee. The company that year was giving away a new Lincoln Continental Mark 111 (with those cool opera windows). The front grill was gold plated, with the word "Saladmaster" written in script across the front. Dealers were given keys that corresponded to their yearly volume of purchases. If one of those keys started the car, it was yours.

You earned the number of keys according to the volume of purchases you had that year. When it was time to see who the winner was, they asked each person with keys to try them out on the Lincoln. Someone said, "Ready...set...go!" It was instant chaos! People knocked over chairs and tables in their eagerness to try their keys—including me.

I will admit to feeling pretty deflated when all of my keys failed to start that gleaming Lincoln. Chris and Alice won that car—and I was (mostly) happy for them.

CROSS COUNTRY

In 1976, we brought the whole family to Boston for a convention. I had just bought my first new motorhome, and it was a class "A", at 26 feet. It was a tight squeeze with Elaine and me and our three boys, and a long, long drive, but we had so much fun.

Somewhere in the Midwest we ran into a storm that was much stronger than anything we were used to in the Pacific Northwest. The sky became very dark—almost black—and rain poured down in torrents—faster than the wipers could clear the windshield. When I felt the wind actually lift the front of our motorhome, I looked over at Elaine and without a word we knew what to do.

It was time to get off the freeway. After a mile or so, we found a rest stop and pulled in.

Even when we had parked, it was still a little scary. The day seemed as dark as night, and the wind shook our motorhome like a little toy. And then it was over. The wind and rain died away, and we went outside to look around. Right to my left, a little Volkswagen bug had snuggled up against our motorhome for shelter. Broken tree branches covered the parking lot. I found out later that I had just survived my first and only tornado. Back on the freeway, we saw cars and trucks literally blown off the road. If we had stayed on the freeway, we would have certainly been one of them.

We arrived in Boston in a driving rain, only to encounter signs that said "No motorhomes allowed," because of the narrow streets. When I called the state police and explained my circumstances, they told me how to find the routes where delivery trucks go. Pretending to be a truck, then, we made it to the hotel.

The head bellhop took pity on us and said we could pull into his private parking space undercover, because of the rain. But they had no place to park a motorhome overnight.

The clerk at the front desk welcomed us, but told us not to walk on the street behind the hotel in the dark, because it wasn't safe. "But it's okay in the morning," he said cheerfully.

After the convention was over, we decided to go home through Plymouth to see a replica of the ship that brought the pilgrims over to our shores. It wasn't a very big vessel for such a long journey across the Atlantic. It made me feel a little ashamed for thinking our motorhome was too confining.

When we came into New York, they turned us away from the tunnels leading to the Statue of Liberty. Instead, we found ourselves in a low-income part of the city. As we approached a stoplight at one of the intersections, there was one car ahead of us. When the light turned green, however, the driver didn't move.

"Maybe I should go and check on the driver," I said to Elaine, "to see if he's okay."

"In this part of town?" she said. "I don't think that's a good idea."

I honked my air horn at the driver. That got some action. He suddenly threw the car into reverse and backed right into me!

Now I had no choice but to get out of our motorhome and see if the driver was okay. When I asked him if he was all right, he just shrugged his shoulders and refused to speak.

Luckily for us, a policeman had watched the whole incident transpire. When the officer came over to question the driver, he got the same response. About that time, a door burst open in a house across the street and a rather large lady came running out of the house, yelling and waving her arms. Pointing at me, she said, "That man just ran into my car!"

The police officer calmly contradicted her. "No," he said, "*that* car just backed into this man's motorhome. Is this your car?"

"Yes!"

"And who is this man sitting in the car who refuses to speak?"

"I've never seen him before in my life!"

He turned out, however, to be her husband, who didn't know how to drive and had no driver's license. We never figured out what he was doing sitting in the car at a stoplight. Apparently, startled by our airhorn, he shoved the car into gear and stepped on the gas. The gear he had chosen, however, was reverse.

We were pleased (and mildly surprised) to learn that this interesting couple actually had car insurance. So with the policeman looking on, we exchanged numbers and went on our way—a little banged up, but no worse for wear.

Passing through Pennsylvania on our way home, we rendezvoused at a rest stop with a couple who were also returning from the Saladmaster convention. They related a funny experience to us. My friend had made a cold contact with a family to do a cooking show in their home, not realizing that they were Amish. He got his first clue when he drove up to the house and saw three buggies lined up inside their three-car garage.

When my friend went to plug in his electric skillet, he found that there were no electrical plugs. He had to quickly adapt to using an oil-burning stove. The dinner came off in spite of the unexpected handicaps. The evening produced no sales, but the customer offered them a place to sleep last night.

"It was a feather bed!" my friend said with a smile. "Best night's sleep I've had in years!"

MORE TRAVEL

I'm often asked, "What was the best Saladmaster incentive trip you've ever been on?" I had ever gone on?

That's easy. It was our trip to South Africa.

Only a small group qualified for this trip, and I was one of them. After clearing customs in Johannesburg, our travel agent advised us not to leave the airport, because it wasn't safe. We were warned about a homeless population that was so poor and desperate they would literally cut your fingers off to get at your jewelry.

We loaded onto our bus and traveled to our hotel located in a safer part of the city. From there, we were given a sightseeing tour of the city. The next day, about a half dozen of us transferred to another airport, boarded a small airplane and flew to another major city.

At a little outpost, Jeeps were waiting to take us to the Krueger National Park, where we would have our evening meal and spend the night. Very early the next morning, we got back in our jeeps to view the wildlife in its natural element. At night, we couldn't leave our bungalow without an armed guard because of the prowling predators.

I will never forget waking up early one morning to the trumpet sounds of elephants. Looking out the back window in the bungalow, and there was the mama and her baby taking a bath. As the day went on, we saw hippos, lions, tigers, water buffalos, and gazelles. I particularly enjoyed watching the monkeys, skipping and scampering around, chattering with their companions.

Another one of the more exciting incentive trips I've been on was a trip to Singapore.

Did I say exciting?

In fact, it was a disaster right from the start.

After we boarded our United flight, we were informed over the loudspeakers that the jet door wouldn't close. The plane sat on the tarmac for hours—with no air conditioning—waiting for the maintenance crew to come fix the door.

Finally, they concluded that it needed a new part—which they didn't have in their inventory, and needed to be flown in from another state. At that point, they unloaded us and bused us to a hotel—without our luggage.

The next morning, they picked us up and bused us back to the airport. Thankfully, there was no TSA back in those days; we simply walked back into the plane. But the door wouldn't close…again. And the part hadn't been installed yet. After another wait, they finally got the door closed and we were on our way to Singapore, with refueling stops in Hawaii and Guam.

Then came the bad storm that morphed into a hurricane.

We bounced all over the sky, and were directed to make an emergency landing in Tokyo. Sherry Whipple, one of the Saladmaster winners, was sitting on my right. As the plane lurched and bounced in the headwinds, she gripped my arm like a vise and yelled, "Larry, pray for me!"—which I was happy to do.

With the wind blowing fiercely across the runway, we landed at an awkward angle and blew out several of the plane's tires with loud bangs. An experienced brush pilot missionary sat on my left, and he shook his head as the plane hobbled to a stop on the tarmac. "We have a great pilot," he said.

"I don't know how he kept the plane upright under those conditions."

With the weather conditions being what they were, there were no planes available to take us directly to

Singapore. We had the choice of taking a flight to Hong Kong then on to Singapore, or wait for a plane to arrive the next day. Elaine and I chose to take the Hong Kong flight, which we did. But when we got there, we had no luggage.

In spite of the many difficulties of that trip, it was something I had really wanted to do. It wasn't the sights of Singapore I wanted to see as much as personally meeting someone I had recently heard about.

Neville Tan had been one of the ten most wanted criminals in Singapore. In his younger years, Neville was a gang member, and was placed on death row for his crimes against humanity. He was in a cell where no visitors were allowed to see him. He only received a small amount of food, because he was on death row. One day, someone slipped a piece of paper on his food tray, and he began to read the opening words of the 23rd psalm.

> *The LORD is my shepherd; I shall not want.*
> *He makes me to lie down in green pastures;*
> *He leads me beside the still waters.*
> *He restores my soul....*[6]

After reading and rereading this magnificent psalm, Neville ended up giving his life to Jesus Christ. As time went on, the guards noticed a dramatic change in his life, and the governor eventually commuted his sentence. He was the first person in Singapore to ever be released from death row. Neville had heard the gospel from his Christian grandfather when he was just a boy. The old man continued to pray for his rebellious grandson through the years, but with no visible change in the boy's life. But the words and prayers of this grandfather finally took root in that dark and hopeless place.

My wife and I had the opportunity to spend a whole day with him and his wife, and to hear his story directly from him. It was one of the most joyful days I can remember.

And it reconfirmed an old and valuable lesson to my heart.

Even the most difficult trips can lead to a happy outcome.

5

LESSONS LEARNED

WE ENCOUNTER RULES AS SOON AS WE ARE ABLE to toddle.

In kindergarten there are rules: Don't push. Don't bite. Don't kick. Don't throw.

Don't mark on the walls with a permanent marker. Rules continue throughout our lives. Don't run a red light in your car. Drive on the right side of the road—unless you happen to be in the United Kingdom or one of her old colonies. Don't yell "fire" in a crowded theater. Don't take things that don't belong to you. Don't cheat on your wife or husband. Rules began in the Garden of Eden when there was only one of them.

Our first parents had total freedom apart from one restriction: Stay away from the tree of the knowledge of good and evil. Here was a whole new world loaded with possibilities and delights down every path and around every corner, and only one restriction for their own good. But you know the sad story, because it is *our* story. They refused to obey the one restriction, and ended up being banished from that perfect, beautiful paradise God had created for them.

Not all rules are good and helpful. Some are excessive and foolish. But without them, life wouldn't be possible at all. Rules are like boundaries. They give shape, structure and definition to our lives, which all of us need to flourish. (Picture a red rose growing up and intertwining itself in a supporting trellis.) We have freedom within certain very important boundaries. Imagine a river that won't stay in its banks, or a fire that won't remain in the fireplace. They are "free," yes, but they are also disasters.

It's good to have guiding rules in the workplace, too. Without that framework, we won't find the success and satisfaction that we long for. Here are a few of the lessons I have learned over the years that have helped me succeed.

STAY FOCUSED

Know where you are going, and don't allow anyone to sidetrack you with shortcuts or promises of "a better way." I've experienced a few of those so-called "better ways," and almost always regretted it. Pie in the sky may sound nice, but it's not the kind of pie you can really eat.

If you know me at all, you know I believe that it's vital to have dreams. But how do you chase those dreams without a plan or a compass or a roadmap? There are just too many timewasting dead-ends out there, and life is too short for that. At Saladmaster, our sales consultants start earning income within a week's time, if they commit themselves to follow the training.

I'm reminded of John Bunyan's classic story, *Pilgrim's Progress*. This was an allegory about a good man's passage through life, with all the ups and downs, twists and turns. It was written in the 1600s and at one time was second only to the Bible in popularity. It tells the story of Christian's journey from the City of Destruction to the Celestial City, atop Mount Zion. There are plenty of obstacles, dangers, and distractions along the way, and reading that book, you sometimes wonder if Christian will ever make it. But in spite of a thousand difficulties, he stays on the path and completes his journey. I've always thought of this story when it comes to dealing with distractions. Don't lose your way and forfeit your dreams!

By the way, I love some of the sayings of this great old author from the past. Especially this one: *"What God says is best, is best, though all the men in the world are against it."* [7]

My bottom line here is this: If you are a Saladmaster dealer or salesperson, don't let some fast talker with "a better deal" entice you off the path of achieving your success through Saladmaster. Don't let people pass out business cards in your office. If you see it happening, escort them politely but firmly out the door. Trying to add on other lines in addition to Saladmaster will become a cancer in your dealership.

KNOW YOUR DREAM

Think it through. Write it down. Create a rough outline of how you plan to achieve it. Have you ever heard of a "dream board"? It's a simple bulletin board decorated with representations of what you would like to obtain or achieve. As I've traveled around the world and visited different dealers, I've seen all kinds of things on dream boards: cars, homes, boats, and posters of exotic locations in faraway places.

There's nothing wrong with having dreams—or even big ones. Small dreams get small results; big dreams get big results. Remember, God will help you if you seek His help with an open, believing heart. Just remember— He may use the opportunity to point you in a different direction. But that's okay. You really don't want to travel any road in life without Him.

I recently heard the governor of New York tell a television audience, "You don't need any help from above." I firmly disagree with that. You do need that kind of help. All of us do. No matter how well intentioned you are or how hard you try on your own, you won't achieve the *life* success you truly desire without the Lord. As the apostle Paul wrote, "For I can do everything through Christ, who gives me strength."[8]

DON'T TRY IT ALONE

When I first started selling Saladmaster, I had no dream of ever building up a big dealership. It wasn't long, however, before I realized that I could never achieve my goals as a "solo act" in the company. I needed to start recruiting others who could work with me, share in my goals, and participate in the success.

I was well into my years with the company, however, before I began bringing the *right* people on board. It's one thing to recruit sales people who come and go, but it is something else to begin forming a real team who will stick around through all the ups and downs.

By the time Vickie Schmidt was established as our distributor, the dealership was really taking shape. I bought property and built a new office, and we worked hard perfecting a good company structure.

That's when the storm hit. It wasn't a tornado or a hurricane (we don't get many of those in Eastern Washington), it was a storm of circumstances—which I won't detail on these pages. By impacting me, the storm took a toll on the whole dealership.

I sold our new office and moved to a smaller place.

Big mistake! And the first of many.

Eventually, the clouds rolled away and we got back on our feet again. As we began to rebuild, we were given the opportunity to recruit a salesperson in Seattle. That opened up a whole new area for us, to the point that we eventually opened up a Seattle office. From there, we walked through another open door in Anchorage, Alaska—then Guam, and then Hawaii. Today we have representatives selling in Hawaii, Seattle, and our main office in Kennewick, Washington.

I shouldn't have panicked and sold our office when we experienced the downturn, because it wasn't long before we needed it again. Helen Keller, who knew something about difficulties and setbacks in life, once wrote: "Do not think of today's failures, but of the success that may come tomorrow. You have set yourself a difficult task, but you will succeed if you persevere. And you will find a joy in overcoming obstacles."[9]

There are storms of all kinds in all of our lives (part of that legacy Adam and Eve left for us). I have seen more than I can count in my 85 years, but I am comforted by this verse I ran across in the Old Testament book of Nahum:

> *The LORD has His way*
> *In the whirlwind and in the storm,*
> *And the clouds are the dust of His feet.*[10]

If the Lord is in the storm with me, I don't have a thing to worry about.

When you consider my background, and the fact that I never even finished ninth grade, divine help is the only explanation that makes sense.

STAY IN THE FIELD

Even at my age, I still do cooking shows. Why? Because I need the money? Not really. What I need to know *firsthand* is the heartbeat of our prospects—what they like, what they want, what they no longer care about or need. It isn't news to anyone that change is sweeping across our world at a faster and faster pace. I don't want to be trying to tackle today's problems and needs with yesterday's solutions and formulas. To know what is happening as a manager, you have to remain hands-on. If you aren't adapting and building and growing, then eventually you will just be a high-paid sales person. And that was not Harry Lemon's dream for Saladmaster. It took me a long time to figure that out.

When Keith Peterson became the company president, with his priority of good communication and feedback with the dealers, the whole picture took on sharper focus for me.

BECOME A GREAT RECRUITER

If you are a small dealership, start by recruiting another "you," and train that person to recruit as well. When you have ten or more salespeople who are delivering five sets per week—in addition to the five sets you are selling—you will have a master dealership in the making.

Ning Devega, one of my very smart distributors in Hawaii, gave me a simple word picture. When I asked how they had built their dealership in that country, she brought it right back to recruiting. "We were recruiting flowers," she said.

Flowers. Not weeds. Bringing the right people on board has everything to do with success, no matter where in the world you are.

Attitude, as I said earlier, will determine your success of failure. As Zig Ziglar famously said, "Your attitude, not your aptitude, will determine your altitude."

God never created you to be a failure. God never intended for you to live a mediocre life.

As a young newlywed, I wanted to have a strong career and provide my wife and future family with a good living. But I didn't know how. I remember attending a motivational meeting in Los Angeles, when I saw a lady in a pink sweater drive into the parking lot in a brand-new pink Cadillac Coupe de Ville. I didn't have any desire to drive a pink Caddy, and I knew having a lot of money wouldn't buy happiness. But as silly as it sounds, seeing that lady motivated me. I knew I could do better. I knew I could reach further. I could climb higher. I could achieve success in my life beyond anything my father or grandfather dreamed possible. And I wanted to do that. For my wife and family.

For myself.

Again, I want to be careful to give God the glory for what I have achieved in my career. Without His grace and help, I don't even like to imagine where I might be. But what a great ride it has been! Through the medium of Saladmaster, I have had the opportunity to touch and change many lives—and I believe for the better.

And to turn that around, my many friends and colleagues at Saladmaster (I call you "family") have touched and blessed my life in a thousand ways.

6

MEMORY LANE

ONE SUNNY DAY IN LATE MAY I DROVE DOWN THE beautiful Columbia Gorge to a meeting in Portland, Oregon. I had just bought a new Corvette Stingray, and had been anxious to try it out on a little road trip. I picked up my oldest son, who was flying in from Boise and also attending the meeting, at the Portland Airport.

As we were having lunch, I asked if he would mind making a short trip with me. I told him that I would like to drive down into the Willamette Valley and see if I could find some of the places where I had grown up.

He was willing to join me on my nostalgic adventure. (But I suspect his main motivation was an opportunity to drive the new Stingray.) Instead of taking Intestate 5, we merged onto old Highway 99 and headed south.

It shouldn't have surprised me, but nothing looked the way I remembered it. As we got closer to my old home, I kept thinking something—anything—would trigger a memory. I felt a little disappointed, but then told myself, *Don't be ridiculous, Larry. It was 70 years ago!*

We drove up to the old farm where I had spent most of my teen years. The old shack where my dad and I had lived was gone. The only thing that seemed unchanged was the pasture where I used to practice my horse riding and dream of becoming a cowboy.

Then, finally, about a half mile further down the road, something triggered a little emotion. I had my son pull the car over as we drove up to the old Assembly of God church campgrounds. I remembered how, as a young boy, I could hear the believers sitting around a big campfire, singing and shouting praises to God. How I loved listening to their heartfelt music on a clear summer night as I sat on the front step of our old shack. Something in me wanted to join them, but I could never quite work up the courage.

My first sales job, at age 12, was delivering *The Oregonian* newspapers to the farm families in the area. My route included the campgrounds and the little town of Brooks. I didn't realize it at the time, but now I know that this job taught me the power of "Why," and the motivation of aiming for a goal and winning.

I remember being strongly motivated by a contest to win the most newspaper subscriptions. The top seller would win a day at the Jantzen Beach amusement park in Portland. At that time, the park boasted a huge roller coaster called "The Big Dipper."

I was determined to win that contest, and as I look back on that experience, I realize that it was my first introduction to door-to-door selling. And I won! The poor kid from Brooks, Oregon won the trip and got to ride on the Big Dipper Everything we do requires a "Why," and that was certainly true in that contest. For some reason, people were motivated to help an eager, sincere kid win a contest and enjoy a day of fun in the big city. I sold more subscriptions in our little town than I would have dreamed possible.

I gave them a "Why," beyond receiving a good newspaper, and they dug a little deeper and said, "Sure, we could do that."

That motivation still works, by the way. People still respond to the desire to help. If your prospect knows a little about your "Why," it could provide an extra motivation to buy, even beyond the obvious quality and value of the product. Take a minute or two to explain what you are trying to accomplish in your sales career. Give them another reason for making the investment.

Will everyone care about your personal details or motivations? Of course not. But a few will. I've seen it happen again and again.

My son and I drove down the main street in Brooks, but again, nothing seemed the same. I couldn't find the street where my friend had lived, or the old brick school building. I couldn't locate the bar where my father had spent endless hours sitting on a bar stool, drowning his sorrows, trying to understand why my mother had run off with another man.

As a boy, I used to sit there with him as he drank, doing my homework. His small weekly wage from working in the hop fields didn't stretch very far, and buying all that booze didn't help one bit. It seemed like I was always hungry. The only meat I can remember was bologna. Or maybe a rabbit or pheasant I was able to kill with my little .22 rifle.

I would sit on a stool with him until he was too drunk to walk, much less drive home. And young as I was, I would have to load him into the old '42 Ford and drive us home. There were no policemen around in those days to see (much less care about) a young boy behind the wheel. The two old gas stations I had known were gone, and a new station had been built across the street.

What I really wanted to find was the old farmhouse where I had lived with my mother and father before she left us. It should have been down a gravel road in what was known as the Lake Labish farming community. But the area is now occupied by a housing development.

My old school was just an empty lot. I had loved that school—not because I learned much there, but because of my friends. For a lonely boy with an alcoholic dad and an absent mother, friends meant everything to me.

I don't know what my son was thinking as we stood there staring at an empty lot, but I experienced an old memory flashing into my mind. I could still see one of my friend's dad driving up to the school in a brand-new Pontiac. Now *that* was a very big deal! It featured the head of Pontiac, the famous Indian chief. And it lit up red at night! My friend was so proud to get in that car, and the rest of us were in awe. His dad owned a dairy not far from the school, and it had apparently prospered.

As we headed out of town I looked in vain for the old drive in movie theater and the hamburger drive in. But they were gone, as if they had never existed. It was a strange, almost melancholy feeling, until I reminded myself that all of those places were in the distance past.

What really matters is today.

The world is changing by the day, and we must accept that. What choice do we have? In our sales world, what was a good presentation or method one year ago may not have any impact at all tomorrow morning.

We need to live each day God gives us to the full.

As I thought about these things, I remembered a quote from a famous missionary, named Jim Elliot. He once wrote: "Wherever you are, be all there. Live to the hilt every situation you believe to be the will of God."[11] Live to the hilt! I like that.

When you look change straight in the eye, you can find reasons to appreciate it. As we drove the freeway back to Portland, I thought about all of those new buildings and new houses in the little town of Brooks. New trees. New flowers. New sidewalks.

Probably a new school or two. Progress everywhere you looked.

And yes, those new families in those new homes certainly need your Saladmaster products in those new kitchens!

7

CLOSING THE LOOP

"**O**KAY, LARRY. HOW DO YOU DO IT?"

People ask me that question all the time. I hear it from dealers, consultants, and people in all sorts of professions. How do you work your way from the bottom, stay at something for 50 years, and make it a success?

Because I've been around so long, I am sometimes introduced as a "legend." That's fine, I guess. People have to say something nice when they are introducing an old-timer. The truth is, if our dealership has climbed the ladder, it's only because I've had phenomenal managers and a wonderful team, and we have achieved it together.

The only title I really want for myself is "Salesman." I am who I am by the grace of God, and that is the bottom line. To become a salesman, stay a salesman, and succeed as a salesman, however, may very well depend on two simple questions:

How do you close the sale?

How do you employ the power of "Why"?

CLOSING THE SALE

One of the questions I get asked most (as you might expect) is, "Larry, how do you close a sale? What have you learned in 60-plus years of direct selling?"

Most of the time, prospective customers delay completing the purchase with one of two statements. They will either say, "It's too expensive," or "I need time to think about it."

As Zig Ziglar used to say, it really boils down to this: "People can't really make a decision for or against your product if they don't have enough information." In many cases, the consultant is in a big a hurry to get to the end of their presentation, so they can ask them to buy the product. In the process, however, they neglect to answer questions and concerns. They don't give enough information for the customer to feel comfortable with making a long-term investment. So the natural answer comes back: "I have to think about it …or sleep on it… or talk to my husband…or I will call you."

Now of course any of those things could be very true. But don't let it be because you haven't given them reliable information and solid reasons for making the purchase.

When the customer says, "I don't think we can afford this," or "I'm not prepared to make a decision now," what they really might be saying is, "I need more information before I make this decision."

At that point, you can either fold up your tent and leave the prospect for another sales person who is more prepared, or you can say, "I can understand that. May I ask what part of the presentation you need to think about? Is it the initial investment, or the monthly investment?" Then you shut up and look right into their eyes, and wait for their answer.

Until you find out what is bothering your prospect or causing him or her to hesitate, you are really in the dark. It might help at this point to go back over the features and benefits of the products—or maybe tell a story about someone who had a tough time deciding to purchase, but then was so glad that they did.

Recently I was training a new person in an in-home presentation. The consultant put on the demonstration with three families present. This trainee had only seen one other show, and had just completed her in-office training. But that's where good coaching comes in. I was with her at that presentation, and had already prepared her with what to do and what to say. Yes, she may have been a little nervous, but she wrapped up the show with flying colors, and all three families invested in our products and went home happy with their purchases.

Did they have hesitations going in? Yes, they did. Did they have questions before they committed to buy? Yes, they did. But she was expecting and anticipating those questions, and answered them with a smile.

One of the reasons so many sales consultant have such a low closing average is because they are afraid to ask the closing question. If you never ask the question, you will never know whether they want to go ahead with the order or have some questions and objections. Don't be afraid of questions! As I said, these queries are one of the ways a customer is saying, "Tell me more." Information—or lack of it—is the highway to success or failure.

So when you're ready to wrap up, you take a deep breath, slowly relax, ask your closing question, and wait patiently for the answer. At this point, it's important to stay quiet. If they want to go forward, great. If they don't, then you need to hear them out and discern the real reason for their "no," or their "I need to think about it." Once they voice their hesitation, then you have an avenue to proceed. Often it is as simple as forgetting a credit card or leaving the checkbook at home, allowing you to easily make other arrangements. Unless and until you know the real objection, you can't overcome the objection.

Always remember that it isn't you they are objecting to, it is the offer. In some cases they simply may not have understood the offer. Just explain it as simply as you know how. You don't have to become a trial lawyer or talk as fast as an auctioneer. Just be pleasant and crystal clear. Go into your presentation with your negative emotions in check and love in your heart. Don't drag yesterday's noes with you into today's presentation.

THE POWER OF "WHY"

One thing I have learned is the power of the simple word "Why." By asking taking the time to ask the prospect why they are choosing not to buy, you will learn the true objection—and have something to work with.

Your prospect has "why" questions, too. Why should I go ahead with this offer? Why should I do it now, instead of waiting? Why should I buy from you, when I could buy from someone else?

I didn't fully understand the power of this word until I read *The Power of Why*, by Tommy Hopkins. If you take the "Why" out, you have no motivation to do whatever you set out to accomplish. "Why" is the fuel that gets you from Point A to Point B.

When you answer your sales prospect's why questions, you open the door for them to make a decision—and feel very happy about it.

"Why," of course, simply means "For what reason or purpose." Why should your prospect buy your product?

Why should they buy it now?

Why should they buy it from you?

Answer those questions, and you are on your way to closing the sale.

I remember when one of my managers wanted to win a jacket. The jacket became her why—her reason to work very hard and reach a certain goal. And she did. It was a little self-motivation that enabled her to reach her objective and win the jacket. In another case a man wanted to buy a new car, but knew he would have to extend himself and push his work habits to a new level to make enough money. The car became his "why" to work harder. As I mentioned earlier, I experienced this as a paperboy selling subscriptions—with my huge "why" of a free day at Jantzen Beach amusement park dancing in my imagination.

I remember how this concept worked in my recruiting efforts in a big way years ago. The lady who is now my general manager had just started as a sales consultant for our dealership, when her former employer came along and was trying to entice her back. In an earlier conversation, I had heard her mention that she and her husband had dreamed of visiting Hawaii. With that in mind, I designed a special contest for that couple: if they reached a certain sales goal in a certain amount of time, they would win a trip to the islands. This became a huge challenge and "why" to her.

She and her husband did win that trip, and now, 31 years later, they work out of a beautiful, spacious office in Honolulu.

Her "Why" had become "Why not?"

8

A QUESTION OF TIME

S EVERAL YEARS AGO I WAS RETURNING FROM ONE OF my many trips and found myself watching a science fiction movie called "In Time" on the video player.

The basic plot takes place in a future world where people stop aging at 25, when a one-year countdown begins, revealed by a device on their forearm. When the number zero, the person "times out" and dies instantly. Time in this strange world has become the universal currency, transferred directly between people or stored in "time capsules." The only way out of the situation is to have the money to literally buy more time—and gain a shot at eternal youth.

The plot is a lot more complicated than that, and adds all sorts of situations that build the tension and the drama. It might be your cup of tea, and it might not. It's not the sort of movie I would normally watch, but in this case, I'm glad I did. What I got out of it was a sharp reminder that time is an extremely valuable commodity that can't be replenished. When it's gone, it's gone. And how you use it is very, very important.

When we are younger, we tend to think we have an endless supply of it. The older you get, the more you are reminded that this isn't true. All of us have a limited supply. And in comparison with eternity, it isn't very much. In the New Testament book of James, the apostle writes:

> Look here, you who say, "Today or tomorrow we are going to a certain town and will stay there a year. We will do business there and make a profit." How do you know what your life will be like tomorrow? Your life is like the morning fog—it's here a little while, then it's gone. What you ought to say is, "If the Lord wants us to, we will live and do this or that." (James 4:13-15, NLT)

Life is brief. Just a puff of mist carried away on the breeze. And on a very, very practical level, this speaks to me about the critical need to manage our time. Every direct salesperson (and everyone else, for that matter) needs to value time as a commodity.

Once it is spent, it will never return.

Everyone in the movie had a sort of watch on their forearms, ticking down their remaining time to live. *Tick, tick, tick.* Some of the characters learn that the only way they can add time back onto the clock is to have more income.

But of course that part is fantasy. Yes, our watches really do count down the hours, seconds, and minutes of our lives. But we can't buy more. Not if we had all the money in the world. Time isn't for sale on eBay or Amazon or the black market, or anywhere else. Whether you are a billionaire, a king, or the poorest man in town, we all get our time allotment from God.

Here is another word from the New Testament that I really like: "Live life, then, with a due sense of responsibility, not as men who do not know the meaning and purpose of life but *as those who do*. Make the best use of your time, despite all the difficulties of these days. Don't be vague, but firmly grasp what you know to be the will of the Lord."[12]

God's Word advises us to use our time wisely because He knows that there are many things in life that can distract us from what truly matters. As I watched that movie on the airplane, I realized (once again) how important it was to not waste time or fritter it away, so that you won't have to look back with regret.

In the direct sales world, you earn by what you do, what you actually accomplish, not just because you showed up. Maybe that's what I've always liked about it. There is no misunderstanding about sales; you either sell product, or you don't; you either recruit good people to work with you, or you don't. You can't fake it or hide behind a college degree or a fancy job title. The difference, day in and day out, week in and week out, is your attitude, and how much time you are willing to put into your profession. Those who habitually and carefully maximize their time and put a little extra into their efforts every day will enjoy a tremendous edge over their competition.

I remember reading about a Lever Brothers salesman in the 1950s who thought about winning and achieving every waking hour. He made Saturdays part of his calling schedule on potential customers, and didn't let rain or snow stop him. He not only became the top sales person in the company, he ended up buying the company—and then went on to buy another company. That is what attitude can do for those who are willing to make the adjustments.

TIME AS CURRENCY

In the movie I spoke of, you could earn time and spend time, just as you would any currency. Time replaces money. When you run out of time, you run out of life. It's over.

That's not too far from our reality, is it?

You and I have been allowed a lifespan, and no one but God knows how long each of us has. Let's say God has allotted you 65 years. That means you have 34,164,000 minutes deposited to your life account. If you make it to 75, that number is 39,420,000. The clock starts ticking with your first breath, and by the time you are 16, you have already used up 8,409,600 minutes of your allotment.

Now these thoughts may seem morbid, but they are actually life-giving. We are reminded that every day God gives us is precious, and every opportunity that opens up to us may never open up again.

In the movie, the people of that society would get up every morning, look at their wrist, and watch the seconds, minutes and hours of their lives ticking down. What would that be like? What if we knew for sure that we only had X number of years—or months—on earth? Personally, I believe there would be some changes in how we would live our lives. We would, as the Bible says, "Be very careful, then, how [we] live — not as unwise but as wise, making the most of every opportunity" (Ephesians 5:15). I have only briefly touched on this movie; I would recommend that you watch it. As you do, ask yourself, "How would I function as a sales consultant in such a world?" I imagine that you might make changes in what you are currently doing. I have a hunch you would put more time into prospecting, and be more diligent with your bookings and asking for referrals. Realizing how much time was worth to you, you would think more carefully about everything you do.

It's not a bad way to live. Because that's our reality, too.

You have limited time to prospect. You have limited

time to schedule cooking shows. You have limited time to make calls and call-backs. You have limited time to follow up on referrals. You also have limited time with God, limited time for travel and personal development, and limited time with your family, friends, and loved ones. Let's face it, we have limited everything. So let's be careful with the time we have, and not assume that we have an endless supply.

We don't.

We never have.

9

PROSPECTING

ONE DAY AS I WAS DRIVING FROM SEATTLE TO Portland, I was listening to the car radio and heard about Bill Porter, a man severely disabled with cerebral palsy who sold Watkins products in Portland, Oregon, door to door. Even though his fingers were so twisted that he couldn't button his own shirt, he became the number one sales person for the entire Watkins Company. And he did it through sheer dedication and determination.

It hadn't been a world class day for me. Okay, let's be honest. It had been a very bad day, and I remember being discouraged over what had happened the day before (which I can't even remember now) and feeling quite sorry for myself. As I listened to Bill Porter's story, however, tears began to run down my cheeks. I found myself saying out loud, "Larry Dickman, you have nothing to feel down about! Are you kidding? Just look at what this man has accomplished in his world with his extreme disabilities! Get a grip!" Right then I began talking to the Lord and repenting for my bad mood and self-pity.

More than anything else at that moment, I wanted to meet this man. So I called the radio station and asked how I could find Bill Porter. They gave me the number of Tom Hallman, Jr., the man who had written about Bill's life in Portland's newspaper, *The Oregonian*. After getting Bill's number, I called him, and asked if he would have dinner with me that evening. I explained that I was a sales representative for the Saladmaster company, was interested in his story, and would only be in town that night.

He agreed—on the condition that he could bring along his helper, Shelly, and her husband. We met that evening at a nice Portland restaurant, and he told me his story. I was so impressed by what he had accomplished in his life that I invited him to be a guest speaker at my next division meeting. Again, he agreed with the provision that he could bring along his helper, since his speech was not very clear—which of course was fine with me.

They came in the winter in the middle of a snowstorm. After the meeting, I paid him and told him he had a wonderful story to tell—and that he should tell it to the world. He followed my advice, and began traveling and speaking around the country. Later, TNT did a movie about him. You can Google his name and watch his story. He passed away in 2013 at the age of 81.

When I met Bill Porter he was living in his mother's home. She had passed away some years back. Bill was unable to gain employment due to his cerebral palsy, but refused to go on disability. He eventually convinced the Watkins company to give him a door-to-door sales job, selling its products on a seven-mile route in the Portland area. In time, he became Watkins' top salesman, and worked for that company for over forty years.

What got my attention was that every day Bill would go out and prospect, no matter how many noes he encountered and no matter how many doors were slammed in his face. If people were rude or abusive to him, he kept a smile on his face and went right on prospecting. In some cases, the driveway up to a house would be so steep that he would have to crawl to the top on his hands and knees. But that didn't stop him. And when homeowners opened the door to him, they found themselves facing a happy, positive man who enjoyed people and knew his products backwards and forwards.

Some years back I was attending a motivational meeting and had the opportunity to meet one of the all-time great motivational speakers, the late Zig Ziglar. Zig had sold Saladmaster for several years, and was on his way to starting his own company just as I was getting started at Saladmaster. During our brief time together, he shared with me something I will never forget.

"Larry," he said, "You were born to win, but to be a

winner, you must plan to win, prepare to win, and expect to win."

These words have been like a burning bush in my mind that never went out. *"To win you must plan to win and PREPARE to win."* If you don't plan, you won't have any goals, and if you don't prepare, you will never reach them. And an indispensable part of preparing is your willingness to invest yourself in prospecting as a daily routine.

THE INDISPENSABLE INGREDIENT

As I mentioned earlier, I began my career selling freezer food—what was known as "The Food Plan." The eventual goal was to persuade people to buy a new food freezer. But to accomplish that, we would sell them frozen foods at (supposedly) warehouse prices. The company gave us a limited number of referrals to follow up on, but it was never enough. Not even close! Very soon I realized that I would need to go door-to-door, explaining our products and asking for appointments and referrals.

Then I started selling cookware to single working girls for their hope chests. Once again, this required seeking prospects and appointments on a daily basis. Again, the company gave us a few referrals, but never enough to ever make a living. You could starve on the number of referrals the company would dole out.

It's still the same today. The companies we work for might provide some names and addresses and phone numbers, but it will never be a number that can sustain us. It will eventually boil down to seeking prospects on our own, using whatever skill, determination (and thick skin) God may provide us with.

Remember this: Once you have made a sale, you have lost your best prospect! One of the first things I was taught by a very successful professional was that I must replace my prospects one way or another on a daily basis, or I will be out of work. If you have no prospects, you have no place to go.

If you want to be successful in the sales world you must simply accept the fact that prospecting is one of the requirements you must do daily, in one way or another.

There are numerous ways of prospecting. You can and should always ask for referrals. You can prospect where you eat, at your bank or at your doctor's office, or go "cold calling" door-to-door, seeking referrals.

What is a prospect? A prospect is a person who has the ability to invest in what you have to offer, and is willing to give you the time to present your product.

Understanding the difference between a *prospect* and a *suspect* is what separates those who make a lot of money from those who just live from one commission to another.

A "suspect" is a name or a referral that you will either

make into a prospect, or set aside because they have no means to invest in what you have to offer.

No one finds prospecting easy. But it is simply part of the job. It's what any of us must do to survive in a sales career. And to be successful at it, you have to work it into your lifestyle, doing it every day. You can make prospecting an opportunity, or a drag, depending on your attitude.

If you genuinely like people—all kinds of people—seeking prospects and referrals can become something of an adventure. Every individual you meet has a life story, with highs and lows, tragedies and triumphs, hopes and dreams. And no two stories are ever alike. And if you talk to enough people, you will find those who are interested in what you have to talk about—or know someone who might be!

I would never make it on a traditional 9 to 5 job, tucked away by myself in some sterile cubicle in a high-rise office building, working all day with my nose to the computer screen.

I like people. I like helping people with great products. I like sales.

I will say it again: Sales is not a place where you can just coast along. To be successful—or to even survive—you will have to grow in every direction: in your sales, in your bank account, and in your experience. You can't just "get by" or "phone it in," as the expression goes. It is a business that you will either love or hate.

I've been blessed, because I love it.

I was speaking recently with a lady who shared my love for the business, and we found ourselves agreeing quite a bit. We agreed that we love what we do so much, we actually have a hard time setting it aside to do other things. We agreed that we were both workaholics, but loved every minute of it. We also agreed that we needed to be more balanced, and take more time to enjoy life.

All of that is true. But it's also true that if you are going to spend most of your working life in a job of some kind, you might as well find one that gives you pleasure. So let's come to this conclusion: Once you allow the business to be part of your way of life, then and only then can you enjoy the fruits of your labor. And once you discover that prospecting is not a chore, it will become a stimulating and exciting opportunity that will lead you to success.

If you are in sales, I would like to challenge you to set aside two hours per day, five days a week, just for prospecting. If you make that commitment, you will never have to worry about an empty appointment calendar.

The secret to becoming a good prospector is to care about people, and take every opportunity to make friends—whether these people end up investing in your products or not.

A very good place to begin prospecting is with the question: *Who do I know?* Who do I know that might be looking for more income and a business opportunity? Who do I know that is health conscious? With the Saladmaster line, I would ask, who do I know who loves creating delicious and innovative meals in the kitchen?

You probably do know people like that. People who say that kitchen is their favorite room in the house. People who would be happy to hear about what you do and the products you represent.

As you talk to people, in the back of your mind you are asking yourself, could this person be someone who might be interested in our products—if not now, then in the future?

Remember to keep your conversation casual and friendly, and never ask questions in a demanding way. Let them talk, and show your *genuine* interest in them. Try to ask questions that will bring a positive answer that leads to your reason for visiting with that person.

Begin with your friends, family, and coworkers, and then branch out from there. Just recently I set aside a day to prospect, and began the day by making a list of those I wanted to see. One of those people was working in our local bank, and I was able to book an appointment with her. I made notes next to each name, thinking through how we met and how they might be interested in learning about Saladmaster. By the end of the day, I had nine appointments to show my product.

In my earlier years I would go prospecting every Monday through Friday for two hours, from 11:30 to 1:30. During that time, I would invariably set four to five appointments.

Prospecting should always be done at every presentation. Always ask the question you are speaking to, "Who do you know who might be interested in investing in these products?" One of the traps that salespeople fall into is becoming so focused on getting a sale that they neglect to ask their prospect for referrals. Most people know ten or more people—right off the top of their head—who might be interested in hearing a presentation.

There are possibilities all around you if you would use the three gifts God gave you:

your eyes, your ears, and of course your mouth to make friends, who could develop into prospects.

I know a lady who is a master at getting referrals from her customers, but hates making cold calls with a passion. She knows that she has to make asking for referrals as an integral part of every appointment. If she neglects this, she will be compelled to make cold calls, and she won't be easy about it and she won't be on top of her game.

Remember this: The sales will come if you have done a good presentation. But if you have also used the occasion to ask people who else might be interested in your beautiful product line, you will be double winner. If they choose not to invest, you are still a winner because you will have a new place to go, a new opportunity, and potential access to a whole new web or relationships and future prospects.

In Og Mandino book's famous classic, *The Greatest Salesman in the World,* the owner of a business sends out Hafid, a newly recruited salesman, into the marketplace to sell a very expensive robe. Hafid doesn't make the sale, but in the process he accomplished something even better: he created a lifelong friendship.

How I love that book. Mandino's philosophy for becoming the greatest salesman is simple: become the best human being. As one reviewer of the book put it: "A great salesman always gives love to his or her customers, and with love comes trust. The power of love is undeniable. It can even turn the worst enemy into a loyal friend."[13]

10

DREAM BIG

I N A PREVIOUS CHAPTER I SPOKE ABOUT SOME WELL-known individuals who had a dream, and refused to allow difficulty, pain, or even devastating circumstances to turn them aside from their goals. In the process, they left us with a legacy.

We spoke about Thomas Edison, who either invented

the first lightbulb or perfected it, depending on which account you subscribe to. As the story goes, a French reporter with a snarky attitude asked the great inventor how it felt to fail 999 times before achieving final success.

Edison answered, "Young man, I have not failed 999 times. I have simply found 999 ways how *not* to create a light bulb." [14]

Is your dream strong enough to overcome all the adversity that will come against you in life? Stuart Scott once said, "Don't downgrade your dream to fit your reality.

Upgrade your conviction to match your destiny." [15]

Taking command of your dream is the first step in achieve anything in life. With the positive winds blowing in your sails, and your compass pointed to reach that new land of opportunity, you must set your course and make a specific plan about how to get there.

If you don't know what you want, you are like a ship with no sail or rudder, at the mercy of random ocean currents.

A few of years ago I was on one of the Master Dealer trips to Australia. One of the fun things planned was to have a sailboat race with some of the other winners. Thankfully, we were paired up with experienced sailing captains, who showed us how to catch the wind and zip through the water along our planned course.

What an exciting day that was! I will never forget it.

When you are racing forward towards your goal with a strong breeze filling your sails, it is exhilarating. But when the wind suddenly drops or changes and the sails hang limp, the boat loses forward momentum. Maybe I'm a bit of a frustrated preacher, because as we sailed, I kept thinking of sailing analogies that describe our lives here on earth. Our sails go limp sometimes, don't they? We're moving along toward our goals, and then circumstances change and we find ourselves stalled—or maybe just drifting. That's the time to make adjustments!

When the wind changed direction on us out in our sailboat, our captain showed us how to adjust the sail to catch the wind and keep moving forward. He must have known what he was doing, because we won the race.

Change is inevitable in life. And it often happens to us when we are unprepared. We had counted on one set of life circumstances, and we suddenly find ourselves in another. It wasn't what we had planned! It wasn't what we had expected! Some people never do recover from such changes, and end up drifting the rest of their lives. It doesn't have to be. With God's help, we can reset our sails, and take whatever advantage we can from our new circumstances.

No matter what happens, you can keep heading toward your goals. You might have to adjust and refine those goals from time to time, but they need to be big enough to keep you moving in a straight line. They also need to be realistic. Some time ago I had a man on my staff in Hawaii who got homesick for his family in the Philippines, wanting to be with them at Christmas.

That was a good goal. But the way he went about it rendered it impossible—and ultimately tragic. He purchased a small kayak with a tiny sail on the front and set out from Hawaii for his homeland. Apparently he had neglected to study his route and to think through the kind of craft and provisions it would take to row and sail across 5,300 miles of Pacific Ocean.

As far as anyone knows, he never reached the Philippines, and was never heard from again. So ye, do make goals, and stick with them. But make sure your goals are realistic and reachable.

How sad it is when people have no goals or direction at all. Some have gone into deep debt getting through college, but even after graduating, still don't know what they want to do with their lives.

A great place to find and sharpen your goals is by asking God, your Creator. He never intended you to be lost or drifting or a failure. You were made for greatness. In the book of 3 John, the author writes: "Beloved, I pray that you may prosper in all things and be in health, just as your soul prospers."[16] The Lord wants you to prosper in every way—not just financially, but in every aspect of your life. But there is a condition here:

you must first have a relationship with the Author of

your life. He is the Source of direction and wisdom, and He will help you formulate the best goals for your life.

Another Scripture verse I love is in the Old Testament book of Jeremiah. At one point the Lord tells His people: "For I know the plans I have for you...plans to prosper you and not to harm you, plans to give you hope and a future. Then you will call upon me and come and pray to me, and I will listen to you. You will seek me and find me when you seek me with all your heart. I will be found by you."[17]

THAT "D" WORD

I remember being so impressed by the sailboat captain in Australia. There he was with a bunch of amateurs on board, and he showed us how to trim the sales, catch the wind, and sail on to victory.

It goes without saying that he wasn't born with those skills. He had to learn them and practice them and put them to work in all kinds of weather. It's the same with a sales career. You can't get very far without discipline and good work habits. In direct sales, there is no such thing as a time clock. You usually don't have someone standing over you, urging you along and telling you what to do. Those disciplines have to come from within.

If we lack discipline (the "D" word), we end up finding excuses as to why we can't go out prospecting or making sales calls every day. We tell ourselves there has to be a better, easier way of getting to our goal. As a result, that sales career we said we wanted begins to drift off course.

It doesn't have to be that way. You can take ownership of the "hard parts" of salesmanship, and end up finding fulfillment in them. The more you begin to enjoy and look forward to making those calls and seeking those referrals, the better you will do.

Your enthusiasm will be infectious.

My youngest son teaches Math to eighth graders in a public school, and he absolutely loves his job. It shows. Parents want their kids to be in his class, and the students get enthused, too (or as enthused as you can be about Math). His dedication shows before the school year ever begins, as he pours himself into his lesson plans. When he gets into the classroom, he can make it fun—because he has done all the hard work of preparation beforehand.

It's always easier—and more rewarding—to do something you love. And if you have strong, realistic goals and develop your skills in reaching those goals, the forward momentum you feel will be exhilarating. This is how a vision of the future turns into a wonderful reality.

Have you raised your dream sails to catch the wind and reach your goals? What skills do you need to sharpen, and what action do you need to take to make faster progress toward those goals? What adjustments do you need to make in your life to catch the wind and keep your momentum? Maybe there are some non-essentials in your life you need to set aside.

What else could bring you more joy than the day when you reach the threshold of your dreams? You will feel like shouting to the world, "I did it!" You will enjoy all the sweet fruits of your labor—those pictures on your "dream board." At age 85, I am still living the dream, and have a vision for growing our company even larger, expanding our offices, and promoting more people into successful careers of their own.

All of those things are very satisfying.

But there is something even more fulfilling than that.

GIVING IT AWAY

Yes, you need to have fun and enjoy life with your family. Sales people work very hard, and when it comes time to cut loose and have some fun and adventure, they need to jump at the opportunity. You also need to wisely invest what you earn, which brings even more income to have fun with.

But it's even better to invest it in people with needs.

I can never get the words of Jesus in Matthew 25 out of my mind. The scene takes place at the end of time, when we stand before Him, the King, to give an account

of our lives. Take a moment to let that picture and these
words sink in.

> "Then the King will say to those on his
> right, 'Come, you who are blessed by my
> Father, inherit the Kingdom prepared for
> you from the creation of the world. For I
> was hungry, and you fed me. I was thirsty,
> and you gave me a drink. I was a stranger,
> and you invited me into your home. I
> was naked, and you gave me clothing. I
> was sick, and you cared for me. I was in
> prison, and you visited me.'
>
> "Then these righteous ones will reply,
> 'Lord, when did we ever see you hungry
> and feed you? Or thirsty and give you
> something to drink? Or a stranger and
> show you hospitality? Or naked and give
> you clothing? When did we ever see you
> sick or in prison and visit you?'

"And the King will say, 'I tell you the truth, when you
did it to one of the least of these my brothers and sisters,
you were doing it to me!'"[18]

Once you have experienced the joy of giving, your
life *will* change. You will still be every bit as motivated
to succeed and climb the ladder, but the benefits

will go so much further than your own possessions and bank account. You will have the satisfaction of seeing your investment save children from disease, feed hungry families, encourage the prisoner, build a clinic, or drill water wells for people in dry, desolate parts of our world.

I love everything I have achieved and earned through Saladmaster. But I have loved helping people in need the most of all.

KEEPING YOUR PASSION

Did you know that people who hold onto their passion and their dreams can live longer than those who are just going through the motions? When you tell yourself that you have outlived your usefulness, the brain begins sending a message to the body that it is no longer needed. The result?

Some people mentally self-destruct.

Some people just give up and die.

The cure? Just hold onto your dreams. And if you can't find your old dreams create some new ones. (While you're at it, make them big.) Connect to your dreams, let the excitement fill your sails, and you will have reason to live longer.

Life can be fun (yes, even at 85) when you know the

plan, connect to the plan, see the plan taking shape, and work in harmony with the plan throughout your life.

Give up the plastic kayak with the tiny plastic sail and get into a boat that will really catch that wind.

11

I CAN DO THIS!

"I CAN DO THIS!"

These are good words to say.

It isn't Pollyanna. It isn't just happy-talk or an empty mantra or phony words meant to fool yourself. In many cases, or even in most cases, it is really true.

The apostle Paul, who had learned to draw all his confidence from God, told his friends, "I can do everything through him who gives me strength."[19]

If you have chosen sales as your field and your career, you can do it. You can!

Just think of the kid who grew up in a one-room shack with an eighth-grade education (that would be me). Remember Bill Porter, severely disabled with cerebral palsy, walking a seven-mile route every day and knocking on every door?

It wasn't easy for me. It wasn't easy for Bill. But who said life would be easy?

You can do this. You can be a success with Saladmaster or another quality product line. And it doesn't hurt to remind yourself of that out loud every day—when you look into the mirror, when you are driving to your office, when you pick up the phone, when you knock at a door.

One of my favorite books in recent days has been *Rhinoceros Success*, by Scott Alexander. In its pages, the author points out the differences between two animals: a common milk cow, and a rhinoceros in the wild.

A dairy cow basically lays around all day to accomplish one thing: produce milk. And they do a very good and efficient job of it. Recently I had a conversation with a man and his wife who have a small dairy farm. He told me how his cows are basically quiet all day, wandering a bit, eating tons of grass, and then lying around and chewing their cuds. But then, ten minutes before it is time to milk them, they start mooing. It's a great system for everyone. The cows are happy to get hay, the farmer is happy to harvest their milk, and we are happy to drink it.

Cows follow each other around day in and day out, sticking with their routine, and never doing or experiencing anything different or exciting.

What a different picture from a charging rhino—a one-ton mass of muscle that can run up to 25 miles an hour.

The author draws comparisons between these two animals and two different approaches to a sales career. You can approach your profession like a cow, plodding along, mostly following others, or you can make yourself into a charging rhino, thundering toward your goals and pushing past all the obstacles.

That's just a brief paraphrase of an excellent book you need to read for yourself.

Years ago my wife and several others won a Master Deal trip to South Africa, where we spent several days at the Kruger National Park Game Reserve. What an experience that was! That is where I first saw a rhinoceros in his natural element. It was quite an eerie feeling to be standing fairly close to this beast—and to notice that we were actually staring at one another. At one point our guide said, "Don't twitch. Don't move a muscle, or he will charge." I found myself wondering, *What happens if I have to sneeze?* I certainly couldn't outrun him. At the 2008 Summer Olympics Jamaican sprinter Usain Bolt ran 23.4 miles per hour in his 100-meter race. On my best day I'm not sure I could have run faster than five. It wouldn't take long for this 2,000-pound beast to catch up to me and send me quickly to heaven.

The rhino is intense, focused, and will not be deterred by whatever gets in his way. And while I do not want to be a rhino, blasting my way through life and knocking things over, we could all do well to learn some of this animal's qualities.

To achieve your goals in life, you will need to focused, passionate, and charge right through the obstacles in your path. Sometimes I will talk to someone new in the profession and they will say, with a sigh, "Well, Larry, I don't think this is the job for me."

When I ask them why, I usually get an answer like this: "Well, I called on three prospects and no one bought anything. And now several of my appointments have cancelled on me, and I can't seem to get any new bookings. I guess I'm no good at this."

That's about the time in the conversation when I quote Churchill again, reminding them to never give up and never give in.

As we talk further, I might remind this discouraged new sales person that they need to use the right words, at the right time, in the right place. You must know your product and your presentation backwards and forwards. You should know it so well that you don't even have to think about what to say next. But even then, that doesn't guarantee instant success. The best sales representative in the world—with all the right words—may miss a sale if he or she happens to be in the wrong place at the wrong time.

But when all three of those elements line up, charge on in like a rhino on caffeine.

You can do it. You really can.

Have you spent time to learn the right words? The right words to open the conversation and the right words to close the sale? Do you have the right words that will get you a follow-up appointment or a referral to someone else who might be interested? There are any number of external distractions or interruptions you might encounter in a call. You can't control many of those things. But you can control your own presentation, making sure you have knowledgeable and persuasive words, and that you speak them with confidence.

One of the biggest faults I have observed is when a sales representative cuts short the presentation because the prospect "has to be somewhere else" or "doesn't have the time." In a situation like that, it's better to reset the appointment. With a smile, tell your prospect that you want to have enough time to give them enough information before deciding for or against your offer.

In my 50-plus years of direct selling, I have learned this valuable lesson: Always assume you have the sale before you ever start your presentation. Approach every opportunity with a positive frame of mind. Believe you are there before you get there.

After all, who *wouldn't* want to invest in high-quality, supremely-practical cookware like Saladmaster? When you assume a sale before you even begin, you may even look a little shocked when the individual declines your offer. This may put your prospect slightly off guard, allowing you to ask an important question: *"May I ask why?"*

Often it is as simple as, "My husband has our card," or "I left my checkbook at home," or "I have two payments left on another purchase." With this information, you can often arrange a follow-up visit or make other arrangements, and keep the contact alive.

Another good reply goes something like this: "Just to be clear in my own mind, what part of the presentation makes you hesitate? Is it the initial investment? The monthly payments?" If you have to walk away from a sale, it's at least helpful to understand the real reason for it.

If you don't practice this assuming-the-sale-before-the-sale discipline, then why not? As Zig Ziglar might say, "Maybe it's time for a checkup from the neck up, and a good, old-fashioned attitude adjustment."

Where are you at in your sales career? Are you on target? Are you on track, or are you just coasting? Are you plodding along like a sleepy dairy cow or charging like a rhino with an attitude?

Can you picture a rhino with confidence issues, stage fright, or a negative mindset? I can't. It seems like they just pick a direction and charge into their day.

I am reminded of the words of Les Brown, one of my favorite motivational speakers. He said, *"Tell yourself that if it's hard, I'll DO hard. I'm unstoppable."* [20]

You can be all you can be—your best version of yourself—if you tell yourself that failure is not an option. If the day becomes long and difficult, keep moving forward, even if all you can manage are a few baby steps.

In the sales world we should always have a mindset that "no matter what happens, I can overcome it. No excuse is acceptable."

Don't let anything stand in the way of achieving your goals. Keep telling yourself, as I said at the beginning of this chapter, "I can do this!"

And here is one final word on that from Les Brown: "Your dream was given to you. If someone else can't see it for you, that's fine. It was given to you and not to them.

It's your dream. Hold it. Nourish it. Cultivate it."[21]

12

THE LAGNIAPPE

AGNIAPPE IS A STRANGE WORD. WHEN YOU FIRST encounter it, you might think it was an exotic musical instrument. Or maybe a fancy tasseled hat worn by Swiss mountaineers.

But it's nothing like that at all. The word is pronounced "lan-YAP." And it can be described as "a small gift given to a customer by a merchant at the time of a purchase." If you want to give it a broader meaning, you could say, it is "something given or obtained gratuitously or by way of good measure."[22]

If you thought the origin of such a strange word might be complicated, you would be right. I read that the word actually entered English from the Louisiana French, adapting a Quechua term brought into New Orleans by the Spanish Creoles.[23] Got that?

I came across a discussion of the word in *Life on the Mississippi*, by Mark Twain. He wrote: "We picked up one excellent word—a word worth traveling to New Orleans to get; a nice, limber, expressive handy word.... They pronounce in 'lanny-yap.' When a child or servant buys something in a shot—or even the mayor or governor, for aught I know—he finishes the operation by saying, 'Give me something for lagniappe.' The shop man always responds; gives the child a bit of licorice root.'"[24]

A lagniappe made the customer happy. It made them feel like they got "something extra" for their investment.

And it still works that way.

In sales, it is this sort of thinking, going the extra mile for your customers, that separates the winners from the losers. Every successful business is strong on customer service. And with this in mind, we are left with this question: What are some of the ways I can serve my customers?

Many times, it will simply mean keeping up with changes in your customer's needs, wants, and expectations. Change isn't fun, and means extra thought and extra work. But if we want to keep that vital connection with our prospects and customers, we have no choice but to embrace it—or perhaps even get ahead of the curve.

What do you offer your buyers as a lagniappe? A piece of licorice root may have worked in the 1830s, but it probably won't cut it anymore. What is the "extra something," what is the "and then some" that will bring a surprised smile to your customers' faces?

Often, it isn't something large or elaborate all. Even

the little gestures count. Here are a few ideas that I have used successfully through the years.

Where possible, send a handwritten thank you card to all your appointments—those who made the purchase and those who chose not to. Thank them for their time, for their interest, and for their listening ear. If they invested, thank them for the privilege of serving and helping them. Just recently one of my appointments called to cancel. After explaining her reason, she said, "By the way, thank you for your card.

Can we book an appointment next month?"

I would always recommend a nice Hallmark card, because it tells your customer that you care more about them than the price of the card. And while you are at it, ask for the gold sticker that goes on the back of the envelope. When they see the sticker, they will be even more likely to break the seal and open the card.

Send your cards and thank you notes to all your contacts and customers as soon as you get back to your office—or better yet on your way home. Yes, you could more easily send an email or text. But most people get dozens of those every day. It is becoming more and more unusual (and therefore special) to receive a card in the mail with a handwritten message.

While you are at it, do something nice for your office help and management. I buy a small flower arrangement or a Starbuck's gift card every now and then for each of our employees in the main office. On other occasions, I will treat several of the employees to lunch—or pay for a dinner and movie with their spouse.

Recently my general manager and I were out shopping around for a new copy machine. We had spoken with two different company representatives, and both had good machines for a similar price. After visiting with the first company, the sales person from the other company called to confirm his appointment with us. We were running late that day, and asked if we could adjust the time. After explaining our problem, the representative said he was happy to make the change.

I was in the office when the sales rep and his manager arrived. Approaching the front desk, they asked our receptionist if she knew who they were and what company they represented. When she gave them the answer they were hoping for, the sales manager thanked her and gave her a very nice gift card! She was completely delighted.

Guess who got the order for the new copy machine?

For the "price" of a gift card and being kind and thoughtful to our front desk lady, the company realized a sale on an expensive piece of office equipment.

That's what I mean about an "and then some" attitude. It is doing something a little bit extra, a little bit out of the ordinary, and a little bit unexpected. A writer I know calls it "paying forward."

Mark Twain loved the concept of that strange word

"lagniappe" so much that he captured it in the pages of a book. He said it had made the whole trip to New Orleans worthwhile.

It doesn't take much to change someone else's whole day for the better.

And it is always worthwhile.

13

"NO MATTER WHAT"

GENTLEMAN JIM" CORBETT WAS PROFESSIONAL boxer and a World Heavyweight Champion back in the 1890s. He was known as the last of the bare-knuckled prize fighters and the only man on the planet to ever defeat the legendary John L. Sullivan. His whole boxing career consisted of just 20 bouts, but he faced off against the best competition in the world at that time. Nine of his opponents would eventually be enshrined in the International Boxing Hall of Fame.

When he was asked what it took to be a world champion, Gentleman Jim replied, "You become a champion by fighting one more round. When things are tough, you fight one more round."[25]

It was his theme throughout his brief but remarkable career. And in those days, fighting "one more round" wouldn't have been easy at all. Corbett was no Hollywood Rocky, fighting 12 rounds with a mouthguard, cushioned boxing gloves, and a cup under silk shorts. Bare knuckle fighting was basic, brutal and bloody—and it went on and on.

I read that the record for the longest bare-knuckle fight was 6 hours and 15 minutes, for a match in Victoria, Australia back in 1855. It went on for 17 rounds before one fighter finally threw in the towel. [26]

Gentleman Jim wasn't big on surrendering. Restating his theme, he said, "Fight one more round. When your arms are so tired that you can hardly lift your hands to come on guard, fight one more round. When your nose is bleeding and your eyes are black and you are so tired that you wish your opponent would crack you one in the jaw and put you to sleep, fight one more round— remember that the man who always fights one more round is never whipped.[27]

In other words, don't give up. Don't let discouragement push you to the side of the road. Keep going, keep trying, and even though success seems like miles away, you will get there before you know it.

One of the best commitments I ever made as a business person was the year I joined the Saladmaster family. I remember it like it was yesterday. Saladmaster President Harry Lemons and I sat down together, and I explained to him that I had been selling another brand of cookware. I told him that if he would let me become a Saladmaster dealer, I would give him my commitment.

He did, and I did.

That commitment has stood for over half a century, and will last until I take up residence on the Other Side. From the very beginning, Harry Lemons stood for trust and integrity, and I wanted to stand for those same principles.

Am I saying you have to stay with one company forever? Of course not. Life changes, priorities change, and circumstances change. But I am saying that if you commit to selling a line of products and that company commits to you, you need to make that commitment solid. Without a commitment, you may drift from this to that to the other and never get into a groove that points toward success. But the moment you make a solid commitment, your world will change and your vision will clear; you will begin to see what you really want in life and how to achieve your goals. When you commit, opportunity will be at your doorstep.

You and I will hopefully never get in the ring to go 17 rounds of bareknuckle fighting. But we will—every one of us—encounter opposition, disappointment, setbacks, and disappointing days on our way to a successful career. Each of us will have to "go one more round" when we are tired or discouraged.

Jesus Himself told His followers, "Here on earth you will have many trials and sorrows; but cheer up, for I have overcome the world."[28]

Several years ago I made a verbal commitment to a

lady in the United Kingdom who had challenged me to write a book about my life. I knew it would be difficult for me. I am a salesman by profession and training, and not a writer. I would need to find a publisher and an editor and figure out how to get it done.

I'm so glad I did. My first book, *A Salesman!* went to press in 2015. No, it hasn't been a runaway bestseller or made the New York Times list. But it has sold over 4,000 copies all over the world, and people are ordering multiple copies to pass out to their sales people. I'm so grateful that British woman challenged me, and I am also glad I made a commitment to her. Without that commitment, I might have thrown in the towel on numerous occasions.

Commitment is only a ten-letter word, but it is powerful. I have committed to my wife in marriage "until death do us part." I have committed to serve my Lord and Savior, Jesus Christ. I have made commitments to my friends, to customers, and to Saladmaster. And those commitments have kept my life on course.

Commitment means, "I will stick with this *no matter what.*"

Does that sound like a serious, grit-your-teeth sort of arrangement? It can be at times. But here is the secret. No matter how challenging that road might become, it leads to the best destinations you could ever experience in life.

One more round is worth it.

14

LOVE YOUR WORK

IKE PLACE MARKET IS A PUBLIC MARKET IN THE heart of Seattle, Washington. It has been open since 1907, covers nine acres, and includes a fresh produce farmer's market and many shops and stalls operated by countless craftspeople and merchants. It is Seattle's most popular tourist destination, with more than 10 million annual visitors.

Oh, and did I mention the fish market? I think that is what most people come to see. It's a real market selling real fish, but the difference lies in how much fun they have doing it. They are best known for their habit of hurling customers' orders across the shopping area. The fishmongers, as they are called, dress in orange rubber coveralls and boots. One calls out an order, and it is immediately shouted back by all the other staff. He might yell out, "Salmon, going to California!" Or maybe, "Crab, bound for Arizona!" The original fishmonger will then throw the customer's fish across the room to a person behind the counter, who will wrap it up with a smile.

That's what makes it fun. There is lots of shouting, joking around and fish flying through the air. In fact, a sign on the wall warns customers, "Caution! Low flying fish!"

Imagine a workplace where everyone chose to make it fun whenever they could! No wonder the tourists flock to watch the show and buy the fresh fish. I read somewhere that the fish market was almost bankrupt in 1986. That's when someone suggested they advertise themselves as "world famous," and start having some fun.

After that, there was no looking back.

Having visited the market on several occasions, I started asking myself, "How could sales representatives learn from what they do?" Obviously, selling fish and selling cookware are very different propositions. No one wants to attend a Saladmaster presentation and see pots and pans flying through the air. Even so, I took away several simple lessons from this unique market.

First, they decided to make it fun. And that changed everything.

Second, they decided to share that fun, to the best of their ability, with their customers.

Third, they had a change of attitude.

Fourth, they began to fall in love with their work, and look forward to coming in every day.

Perhaps one of the reasons we lose sales people is because they have never had the opportunity to have fun with what we do—or maybe some of us old timers have never showed our new representatives how much fun it could be.

Cooking shows are a lot of work. But that's only half of it. When I am putting on a cooking show, I like to invite my guest to help cook the meal—and I try to make sure we have fun doing it. I will have someone time the pineapple upside down cake baking on the stovetop, or put the chicken in the electric skillet, showing them a way to do it with no splatters. Questions—all kinds of questions—pop up, and we keep talking and sharing and laughing while the food cooks.

What is better than smiles and laughter in the kitchen, surrounded by the wonderful aromas of fresh food?

Why are kitchens so often the favorite room of every home? It's because the family likes to gather there. Most people like to talk while they are cooking a meal or cleaning up. It's a good time to share with loved ones about your day or laugh over a funny incident. And everybody likes good food.

Why shouldn't a cooking demonstration be fun?

Why shouldn't talking about a product line you believe in be enjoyable?

Many years ago, I made the choice that I would love what I do, and do what I love. You might not have a choice about the kind of work you can do, but you can always choose the energy and optimism you bring to your work. You can always choose your attitude. If you choose to be impatient or grouchy, you will live with the consequences of that negative mindset.

Look for ways to engage your prospects or referrals. If they see that you enjoy what you do and believe in what you do, they may be more ready to hear what you have to say.

Earlier in the book I spoke about being a people person and liking all sorts of people. If you genuinely like and care about someone, they will sense it immediately. Most people will also be able to sense if you are faking it, or just rehashing a script like a robot.

If people have a good time at your cooking shows, word will get around. Your prospects will invite you back, and their friends will invite you, too.

The more you fall in love with what you do, the more you will want to do it, and the more you will want to continue in the business. People often ask me, "Larry, when are you going to retire?" (They have been asking me this for about 20 years now.) To my way of thinking, I already retired about 51 years ago. It happened when my job became a passion. It happened when I started loving what I do, and looking forward to what I might accomplish.

Besides that, Saladmaster has become a second family to me, and why would you want to leave family?

The bottom line is that having fun in your chosen profession is also the best road to succeeding in that profession.

And that is no fish story.

APPENDIX

More Names that Make Me Smile

At age 85, my memory isn't what it used to be.

But it isn't bad, either.

Part of what keeps the circuits popping is remembering the names of some of the wonderful people I have worked for, with, and beside through the years.

On our recent Master Dealer trip to Peru, Wayne Fritz, Carolyn Evans, and I begin reminiscing about some of the wonderful times we have had in our careers in Saladmaster, and the many people with whom we have shared this journey.

In this chapter, I'd like to introduce you to some of my personal heroes.

CHRIS NATHATIS

I mentioned Chris in an earlier chapter. He was an early dealer in the Boston area, and made a name for himself doing Saladmaster informercials on local television. I remember so well visiting Chris and Alice in their historic home, a former governor's residence. Chris's magnificent home was a symbol of his well-earned, well-deserved success, and included a full-size tennis court and swimming pool. A live band played dinner music while we all enjoyed the feast of a lifetime. And later... dancing!

GENE LEWIS

I met Gene in Yakima, Washington in my early days at Saladmaster. Gene was training a new dealer at the time, and the regional manager invited me to come and learn about cooking a Saladmaster dinner. When I saw him make a salad, I was blown away!

Feeling a little overwhelmed by what I was watching, I told the regional manager that I would never learn to do a dinner like that—much less learn how to operate that salad device. Noticing the Band-Aids on the trainer's fingers, I was even more convinced that dexterity with that machine was way beyond my pay grade. But I couldn't stop watching. The way he prepared those vegetables was amazing to me—like nothing I had ever seen. Everyone watching the demonstration wanted to buy one. "Larry," I told myself, "you *will* learn how to do that. You *will* become a Salad Master! And I guess I did.

HANK BLOOM

The very first Saladmaster trip I earned was to Hawaii. Hank Bloom was the event coordinator for the company who set up all the travel at that time. Later on, as the company grew, they contracted with Illinois Travel, owned by David Sepenic.

IRVIN TUREK

Years ago, I was excited to learn that Elaine and I might win a Saladmaster trip to Hawaii. Wow! That was a really big deal—and hugely motivational to me. I remember wanting to go on that trip for several reasons. First of all, I had a friend and fellow dealer who kept encouraging me, insisting that I could do it. "Give it a try, Larry!" he kept saying. "I think this will be an exciting trip." His name was Irvin Turek, and over the years Elaine and I became friends with him and his wife, Phyllis.

My second reason involved a delinquent account in Hawaii; I really needed to show up in person and find out what was going on. My third reason was…just because I wanted to! When I was in the Navy, I had spent one afternoon on Waikiki Beach on the way to my first duty station in Japan. And one little taste of Honolulu is enough to make you dream about having more.

After collecting my product from the bad account and getting that out of the way, Elaine and I could relax and enjoy the scenery on the H-1 highway. Looking up to my left, I caught a glimpse of all the lovely homes on a green hillside.

"Someday," I told Elaine, "I'm going have an office here." I was just dreaming out loud, I think, and didn't really believe it would ever happen.

But that was one dream of many in my career that came true.

GIL FLOCKER

After Harry Lemons retired, a man named Gil Flocker became president of Saladmaster. Some years later, Harry sold the company to a businessman named Jeff Dyke. As I recall, Jeff appointed Harold Curtis as president. But Mr. Dyke's term was sadly cut short when he died in an airplane crash in Mexico.

Eventually, the company was sold to the Regalware company, who are owners to this day. They own the Saladmaster trademark, and manufacture the Saladmaster line.

SO MANY OTHERS....

Some of the early dealers when I started my career were Chris Nathatis, Mark Benson, Joe Richardson, the Walker family. (There were too many to name them all.) One of the best prospectors was Mama Walker's son, Preston. Another son, Claude Walker, later changed his career and got into politics. I also remember Phil and Janet Jensen in South Dakota, who also went into politics. And I can't forget my great friend, Rickie Musset.

Bill Francisco, who was the Vice President of Saladmaster for several years Bill became my close friend and mentor. Bill was one of the first people to set me down and talk to me about focus. "Don't get sidetracked, Larry," he would tell me. "If you keep your eyes on the goal, you will make a success of this." Knowing that I was a country boy, he used to say, "Put blinders on—like you would put on a horse that's pulling a wagon." I knew what he meant. A horse has great peripheral vision, and can become distracted or even panicked by what is passing on either side of him. With blinders on, he keeps pulling that wagon straight ahead.

Keith Peterson took the reins of Saladmaster at a crucial time. From my point of view, the company was at crucial juncture, where it could really take off or lose ground and fall back. Keith accepted the challenge, knowing what he was facing. He committed to build Saladmaster into a recognized leader in the industry, and he took the necessary steps to make that happen.

He brought Garry Robison on staff knowing that he could depend on him to support his commitment. It was a good choice. Today Saladmaster is recognized as a world leader with offices all the world.

Pidoy Pacis committed to build the global Filipino market, and he has accomplished that to the fullestextent.

Ayo Aolaseinde joined Saladmaster to build the market in the United Kingdom.

He started like everyone else, learning to fry chicken and bake a cake on a stove top.

Ayo didn't need a job. He had already been very successful in many other pursuits. But the thought of changing people's lives and improving people's healthy by the way they cook caught his attention. He is now in the president's chair of Saladmaster, and is not only carrying on, but building this company stronger and expanding to areas many of us never dreamed possible. To this day, he is a true builder and a great leader.

My Regional Vice President James Tantiea has committed to build our region, and from what I see he is on his way to greatness, and fulfilling his commitment.

These are some of the names I like to remember. I have learned from their commitment and their determination to build a business—and build a life.

This commitment has been more than just words. Words are cheap. You can even teach a parrot to say words. The kind of commitment I am talking about is one of the heart and soul.

ENDNOTES

1   Genesis 1:7-8, GOOD NEWS TRANSLATION
2   https://quoteinvestigator.com/2011/09/29/you-did
3   https://www.azquotes.com/author/6852-Lou_Holtz
4   https://www.britannica.com/biography/Zig-Ziglar
5   https://www.brainyquote.com/quotes/yogi_berra_621245?src=t_
    nervous
6   Psalm 23:1-3, NKJV
7   https://www.goodreads.com/quotes
8   Philippians 4:13, New Living Translation
9   https://www.wow4u.com/overcomingobstacles/
10 Nahum 1:3, NKJV
11 https://www.goodreads.com/quotes/12747-wherever..
12 Ephesians 5:15-17, PHILLIPS
13 https://booksandmore.blog/the-greatest-salesman-in-the-world-
    book-summary
14 https://instituteforleadershipfitness.com/2012/02/learning-from-
    failure
15 https://www.allcupation.com/motivational-quotes
16 3 John 2, NKJV
17 Jeremiah 29:11, NIV
18 Matthew 25:34-40, NLT
19 Philippians 4:13, NIV
20 https://everydaypower.com/les-brown-quotes-motivation/
21 https://everydaypower.com/les-brown-quotes-motivation/
22 https://en.wikipedia.org/wiki/Lagniappe
23 https://en.wikipedia.org/wiki/Lagniappe
24 Mark Twain, *Life on the Mississippi*

25 en.wikipedia.org/wiki/James_J._Corbett

26 *"The Victoria Ring", Bell's Life in Sydney and Sporting Reviewer,*
    December 22, 1855

27 https://www.azquotes.com/author/3271-James_J_Corbett

28 John 16:33, THE LIVING BIBLE